ALL-TIME-FAVORITE RECIPES

From

Texas

COOKS

Dedication
For every cook who wants to create amazing recipes
from the great state of Texas.

Appreciation
Thanks to all our Texas cooks who shared
their delightful and delicious recipes with us!

Gooseberry Patch
An imprint of Globe Pequot
246 Goose Lane
Guilford, CT 06437
www.gooseberrypatch.com
1 800 854 6673

Copyright 2019, Gooseberry Patch
978-1-62093-345-9

Do you have a tried & true recipe...tip, craft or
memory that you'd like to see featured in a
Gooseberry Patch cookbook? Visit our website at
www.gooseberrypatch.com and follow the easy steps
to submit your favorite family recipe.

Or send them to us at:

Gooseberry Patch
PO Box 812
Columbus, OH 43216-0812

Don't forget to include the number of servings your
recipe makes, plus your name, address, phone
number and email address. If we select your recipe,
your name will appear right along with it... and you'll
receive a FREE copy of the book!

TEXAS COOKS

THE LONE STAR LEGACY

From cowboys with chuck wagons for making grub out on the range to sophisticated fare these days in cosmopolitan cities, Texas has it all. As our biggest continental state, it has enough room to dish up a variety of tastes to satisfy almost any palate.

Food specialties in cities vary one to another. Special areas include west Texas, focusing on beef, and the Gulf Coast, where seafood specialties rule. Don't forget the Rio Grande Valley, where Ruby Red grapefruit grows. There's eastern Texas, so reminiscent of the Deep South, where catfish and collard greens are staples, and Hill Country, relishing in German specialties, along with peaches and pecans. Plus, there's south central Texas, around Austin and San Antonio, where Tex-Mex and barbecue are foodie favorites...and don't forget all the classics that start with C...cheese enchiladas, chili (without beans, of course), chicken-fried steak, catfish in cornmeal batter and chile con queso.

And the amazing cooks from the Lone Star state that have shared their recipes in this Gooseberry Patch cookbook are equally as varied in the recipes that they share...recipes that are dear to their hearts. You'll find everything from Buttermilk Cinnamon Rolls and Egg & Bacon Quesadillas to Toss-It-Together Salsa and Barbecue Pork Ribs. We know you will love this collection of tried & true recipes from cooks from all around the great state of Texas. Enjoy!

OUR STORY

Back in 1984, our families were neighbors in little Delaware, Ohio. With small children, we wanted to do what we loved and stay home with the kids too. We had always shared a love of home cooking and so, **Gooseberry Patch** was born.

Almost immediately, we found a connection with our customers and it wasn't long before these friends started sharing recipes. Since then we've enjoyed publishing hundreds of cookbooks with your tried & true recipes.

We know we couldn't have done it without our friends all across the country and we look forward to continuing to build a community with you. Welcome to the **Gooseberry Patch** family!

JoAnn & Vickie

TABLE OF CONTENTS

CHAPTER ONE

BRING-IT-ON
Breakfast

ENJOY THESE TASTY

BREAKFAST RECIPES THAT WILL

BRING YOU TO THE TABLE WITH

A HEARTY "GOOD MORNING!"

AND CARRY YOU THROUGH THE

DAY TO TACKLE WHATEVER

COMES YOUR WAY!

SOUTHWEST-STYLE SKILLET CORNBREAD

DOUG FERGUSON
NEW BRAUNFELS, TX

This is a recipe I have had for years. I started out with a recipe I got from a friend and customized it to make it my own. I have never seen anything like it! The cast-iron skillet is a must...it's just not the same without it!

3/4 c. onion, chopped
2 6-1/2 oz. pkgs. yellow cornbread mix
1 t. baking powder
3 eggs, beaten
2/3 c. milk
10-oz. can diced tomatoes with habaneros, drained
1 c. frozen corn, thawed
1 c. shredded Cheddar cheese
4 T. oil, divided

1 Place chopped onion in a microwave-safe glass measuring cup. Microwave on high for 2 minutes; cool. Combine cornbread mixes and baking powder in a large bowl. Add onion and remaining ingredients, reserving 2 tablespoons oil; stir until moistened. Let batter stand for about 10 minutes.

2 Add reserved oil to a large cast-iron skillet. Place skillet in oven; preheat to 400 degrees. Remove hot skillet carefully from oven; pour batter into hot skillet. Bake at 400 degrees for 30 minutes, or until golden.

Makes 8 to 10 servings

BENSON'S ULTIMATE PANCAKES

TRIANN BENSON
PLANO, TX

The entire family will ask for more of these amazing pancakes!

1 Combine first 8 ingredients in a large bowl; mix well and set aside. Beat egg whites with an electric mixer at high speed until stiff peaks form. Gently fold into batter. Pour batter by 1/3 cupfuls onto a greased hot griddle.

2 Spoon several blueberries on top of just-poured batter. Cook until bubbles appear on the surface; flip and continue cooking for 2 to 3 more minutes, until golden. Garnish as desired.

Makes about one dozen, serves 6

1-1/2 c. all-purpose flour
1 T. baking powder
1 T. sugar
1 t. salt
1-1/4 c. milk
1 egg yolk, beaten
2 T. butter, melted
1 T. vanilla extract
2 egg whites
1-1/2 c. blueberries
Garnish: maple syrup, whipped topping and/or blueberries

KITCHEN TIP

Frying up a skillet of bacon for breakfast? If there's no spatter guard handy, a large sieve can do the job...just place it face-down over the skillet.

BROWN BUTTER-BUTTERMILK SYRUP

LISA LANGSTON
CONROE, TX

An old-fashioned homemade syrup you will love. Serve with waffles, pancakes, French toast...even cake and ice cream! This syrup goes really well with cinnamon cake and apples or pears.

1/2 c. butter
3/4 c. sugar
1/2 c. buttermilk
1 t. baking soda
1 t. vanilla extract

1 In a small saucepan, melt butter over medium-low heat. Cook, swirling occasionally, until butter turns dark golden. Skim off foam; remove from heat. Pour into a bowl to stop the cooking, leaving any burned sediment behind. Combine butter, sugar and buttermilk in a large saucepan; mixture will bubble up. Cook over medium heat, whisking until sugar dissolves. When mixture starts to boil, carefully whisk in baking soda and vanilla. Cool; refrigerate syrup up to 2 weeks. Reheat before serving.

Serves 4 to 6

FIESTA CORNBREAD

KATHRYN HARRIS
LUFKIN, TX

If you'd like, shred Pepper Jack cheese and substitute for the Cheddar...it will add more kick!

1 c. cornmeal
1 c. buttermilk
8-oz. can creamed corn
2 jalapeño peppers, chopped
1/2 t. salt
3/4 t. baking soda
2 eggs, beaten
1 onion, chopped
1/4 c. oil
1 c. shredded Cheddar cheese, divided

1 Combine first 8 ingredients; set aside. Heat oil in an 8" to 10" cast-iron skillet; pour in half the batter. Sprinkle with half the cheese; pour remaining batter over top. Sprinkle with remaining cheese; bake at 400 degrees for 30 minutes.

Serves 6 to 9

BUTTERMILK CINNAMON ROLLS

**DOBIE HILL
LUBBOCK, TX**

These no-yeast rolls are super easy and fast to make and are always a treat!

1 In a large bowl, combine flour, baking powder, baking soda and salt; cut in cold butter until crumbs form. Stir in buttermilk until well blended; knead dough on a lightly floured surface for 4 to 5 minutes.

2 Roll out to 1/4-inch thickness; spread softened butter over dough to edges. In a small bowl, mix sugar and cinnamon; sprinkle over dough. Roll up jelly-roll style; cut into 1/2-inch slices. Place on 2 greased baking sheets; bake at 400 degrees for 10 to 12 minutes.

Serves 15

3 c. all-purpose flour
4 t. baking powder
1/4 t. baking soda
1 t. salt
1/2 c. cold butter
1-1/2 c. buttermilk
1/4 c. butter, softened
1/2 c. sugar
1 t. cinnamon

MORNING DELIGHT

**JANE WHITE
KOUNTZE, TX**

So delicious and easy to make...no one can resist it!

1 Press one tube of crescent rolls into the bottom of a greased 13"x9" baking pan; seal seams. Set aside. Mix cream cheese, egg, extract and sugar in a bowl; spread over rolls in pan. Top with remaining crescent rolls; sprinkle to taste with sugar and cinnamon. Bake at 350 degrees for 20 to 25 minutes, until golden. Top with sliced bananas, if desired.

Serves 6 to 8

2 8-oz. tubes
  refrigerated
  crescent rolls,
  divided
2 8-oz. pkgs. cream
  cheese, softened
1 egg, beaten
1 T. almond extract
1 c. sugar
Garnish: sugar,
  cinnamon to taste
Optional: sliced
  bananas

CHEDDAR-DILL CORN MUFFINS

VICKIE
GOOSEBERRY PATCH

These dressed-up corn muffins are scrumptious and simple to make.

1 c. cornmeal
1 c. all-purpose flour
1/3 c. sugar
2-1/2 t. baking powder
1/2 t. baking soda
1/4 t. salt
1 egg
3/4 c. skim milk
1 c. shredded sharp Cheddar cheese
1 c. corn, thawed if frozen
1/4 c. butter, melted
3 T. fresh dill, minced, or 1 T. dill weed

1 In a large bowl, mix cornmeal, flour, sugar, baking powder, baking soda and salt; set aside. In a separate bowl, whisk together egg and milk; stir in remaining ingredients. Add egg mixture to cornmeal mixture; stir just until moistened. Spoon batter into 12 greased or paper-lined muffin cups, filling cups 2/3 full.

2 Bake at 400 degrees for about 20 minutes, until golden and a toothpick inserted in the center tests clean. Cool muffins in tin on a wire rack for 10 minutes before turning out of tin. Serve warm or at room temperature.

Makes one dozen, serves 12

 TEXAS TRIVIA

In Texas, as in other states where there are towns started by Czech immigrants, there are kolaches, pastries with fruit fillings, such as peach, prune, cherry or poppy seed. But in the area around the small town of West, Texas, there are also other versions, too. There are savory kolaches, filled with eggs, sausage, bacon or other meats and cheeses, for a hand-held breakfast or lunch treat.

EGG & BACON QUESADILLAS

JOSHUA LOGAN
CORPUS CHRISTI, TX

I make these quesadillas on weekends when I have plenty of time to enjoy them. Serve with a cup of yogurt or some fresh fruit.

1 Lightly spread about 1/4 teaspoon butter on one side of each tortilla; set aside. In a bowl, beat eggs and milk until combined. Pour egg mixture into a hot, lightly greased skillet; cook and stir over medium heat until done. Remove scrambled eggs to a dish and keep warm. Melt remaining butter in the skillet and add a tortilla, buttered-side down.

2 Layer with 1/4 of the cheese, 1/2 of the eggs and 1/2 of the bacon. Top with 1/4 of the cheese and a tortilla, buttered-side up. Cook about one to 2 minutes on each side, until golden. Repeat with remaining ingredients. Cut each into 4 wedges and serve with salsa and sour cream, if desired.

Serves 4

2 T. butter, divided

4 8-inch flour tortillas

5 eggs, beaten

1/2 c. skim milk

8-oz. pkg. shredded Cheddar cheese

2 slices bacon, crisply cooked and crumbled

Optional: salsa, sour cream

EMMA'S GINGERBREAD MUFFINS

BERNADETTE DOBIAS
HOUSTON, TX

If you like gingerbread cookies, you will love these yummy muffins!

3/4 c. butter, softened
3/4 c. sugar
3 eggs
1/2 c. molasses
2 T. light corn syrup
3 c. all-purpose flour
2 t. cinnamon
2 t. ground ginger
1 t. nutmeg
1 t. baking soda
1 c. buttermilk

1 Place butter in a large bowl. Beat with an electric mixer at medium speed until creamy. Add sugar; beat just until combined. Add eggs, one at a time, beating after each addition. Add molasses and corn syrup; beat just until blended. Sift together flour and spices.

2 Dissolve baking soda in buttermilk; add the milk mixture to butter mixture alternately with flour mixture, stirring just until combined. Fill greased and floured muffin cups 2/3 full. Bake at 350 degrees for 15 minutes, or until a toothpick inserted in center comes out clean.

Makes 2-1/2 dozen

TIME SAVER

Use natural paper cupcake liners when baking your muffins. The clean-up is easier when it is time to wash the muffin cups.

FRENCH BREAKFAST PUFFS

LISA STANISH
HOUSTON, TX

These are my mother's mini muffins...they're a wonderful treat with a cup of hot tea.

1 In a large bowl, blend 1/3 cup butter and sugar. Add egg and mix until fluffy. In a separate bowl, stir together flour, baking powder, nutmeg and salt. Gradually add flour mixture to butter mixture, alternating with milk. Fill greased mini muffin cups 2/3 full. Bake at 350 degrees for 15 minutes, or until golden. Remove from muffin cups and roll first in remaining butter, melted, then in Cinnamon-Sugar.

Makes 4 dozen

In a small bowl, mix ingredients together.

2/3 c. butter, divided
1/2 c. sugar
1 egg, beaten
1-1/2 c. all-purpose flour
1-1/2 t. baking powder
1/4 t. nutmeg
1/2 t. salt
1/2 c. milk

CINNAMON-SUGAR:
1/2 c. sugar
2 T. cinnamon

HUEVOS RANCHEROS TO GO-GO

TONYA SHEPPARD
GALVESTON, TX

All the yummy ingredients are wrapped up in a handy tortilla.

1 Lightly coat a skillet with non-stick vegetable spray and place over medium heat. Pour salsa into skillet; bring to a simmer. With a spoon, make 4 wells in salsa and crack an egg into each well, taking care not to break the yolks. Reduce heat to low; cover and poach eggs for 3 minutes.

2 Remove skillet from heat and top eggs with cheese. Transfer each egg with a scoop of salsa to a tortilla. Garnish with sliced avocado.

Serves 2 to 4

2 c. green tomatillo or red salsa
4 eggs
1/2 c. crumbled queso fresco or shredded Monterey Jack cheese
4 8-inch corn tortillas
Garnish: sliced avocado

SPRIGHTLY BREAD

**KRISTIN STONE
LITTLE ELM, TX**

I love, love, love beer bread. But, I don't love beer. I finally came up with a solution...why not use lemon-lime soda? This quick bread is a perfect accompaniment to soups. We love to eat it in the fall!

2-1/2 c. self-rising flour
3 T. sugar
1 egg, beaten
12-oz. can lemon-lime
   soda
1 T. butter, melted

1 Combine flour, sugar, egg and soda in a bowl. Stir well and pour into a greased 9"x5" loaf pan. Drizzle melted butter over batter. Bake at 350 degrees for about 45 minutes, until top is cracked and golden.

Makes one loaf

BEER BREAD

**KIM HINSHAW,
CEDAR PARK, TX**

When I was growing up, my grandma made yummy homemade bread. This version is quick & easy!

3 c. self-rising flour
12-oz. can regular or
   non-alcoholic beer,
   room temperature
1/4 c. sugar
1/2 c. butter, melted

1 Combine flour, beer and sugar in a large bowl. Stir just until moistened. Pour into a greased and floured 9"x5" loaf pan. Drizzle with melted butter. Bake at 375 degrees for 45 to 55 minutes. Serve warm.

Makes one loaf

CHUCKWAGON BREAKFAST SKILLET

JO ANN
GOOSEBERRY PATCH

For a head start on this hearty, delicious breakfast, the potatoes can be cooked ahead of time.

1 Add potatoes to a saucepan of boiling water. Cook over medium heat for 12 to 15 minutes, until tender; drain. Meanwhile, in a large skillet over medium heat, cook bacon until crisp. Remove bacon to a paper towel; reserve some of drippings in skillet.

2 Add potatoes and one to 2 tablespoons oil to skillet; sauté until golden. Add pepper, onion, mushrooms, salt and pepper; sauté until vegetables are tender. Drain; stir in bacon. Top with cheese; reduce heat to low. In a separate skillet over medium heat, scramble or fry eggs in butter as desired. To serve, spoon potato mixture into a large serving dish; top with eggs. Garnish as desired.

Serves 6 to 8

2 lbs. potatoes, peeled and cubed
1/2 lb. bacon, chopped
1 to 2 T. oil
1 green or red pepper, sliced
1 onion, sliced
2 c. sliced mushrooms
salt and pepper to taste
2 c. shredded Colby cheese
2 T. butter
8 eggs
Garnish: fresh chives or parsley, chopped

BLUE RIBBON IDEA

A fun centerpiece for the breakfast table! Thread doughnut holes on long wooden skewers and arrange in a vase for easy serving. Yum!

TEXAS TOADS IN THE HOLE

ELIZABETH HOLCOMB
CANYON LAKE, TX

What better way to get your eggs and toast together? The kids will love this fun version of an old favorite.

2 T. butter
4 slices Texas toast
4 eggs
salt and pepper to taste
Optional: jam, jelly or
   preserves

1 Spread butter on both sides of Texas toast. Using a biscuit cutter, cut a circle out of the middle of each slice of toast; set aside rounds. Place toast slices in a large, lightly greased skillet over medium heat; break an egg into each hole. Season with salt and pepper.

2 Cook until egg white begins to set, then carefully flip. Continue to cook until eggs reach desired doneness. In a separate skillet, toast reserved bread rounds. Top rounds with jam, jelly or preserves, if desired. Serve with toast slices.

Serves 4

LONE STAR BREAKFAST CASSEROLE

SUZANNE FRITZ
ROUND ROCK, TX

Our family loves this easy-to-make breakfast. I have also taken it to potlucks and everyone wants the recipe.

8-oz. tube refrigerated
   crescent rolls
1 lb. ground pork
   sausage, browned and
   drained
1 c. mushrooms, sliced
12-oz. pkg. shredded
   Monterey Jack cheese,
   divided
6 eggs, beaten
10-3/4 oz. can cream of
   onion soup

1 Arrange rolls in the bottom of an ungreased 13"x9" baking pan; cover with sausage, mushrooms and half of the cheese. Set aside. Mix eggs and soup; pour over cheese. Sprinkle with remaining cheese; bake at 350 degrees for one hour.

Serves 8

  - - - - - - - -

SWEET POTATO CORNBREAD

VICKIE
GOOSEBERRY PATCH

The beautiful orange color of the sweet potato makes this bread as pretty as it is yummy!

1 Whisk together all ingredients just until dry ingredients are moistened. Spoon batter into a greased 8" cast-iron skillet or pan. Bake at 425 degrees for 30 minutes, or until a toothpick inserted in center comes out clean.

Makes 6 servings

2 c. self-rising cornmeal mix
1/4 c. sugar
1 t. cinnamon
1-1/2 c. milk
1 c. cooked sweet potato, mashed
1/4 c. butter, melted
1 egg, beaten

RISE & SHINE BREAKFAST SOUFFLE

LYNDA MCCORMICK
BURKBURNETT, TX

A quick-to-fix overnight casserole.

1 Mix sausage, eggs, milk, mustard, bread, cheese and soup in a bowl; spoon into a greased 13"x9" baking pan. Cover; refrigerate overnight.

2 Remove from refrigerator 30 minutes before baking; set aside. Combine cereal and butter; sprinkle over egg mixture. Bake at 350 degrees for one hour.

Serves 8 to 10

1 lb. ground pork sausage, browned and drained
9 eggs, beaten
3-1/2 c. milk
1 t. mustard
6 to 8 slices bread, cubed
1-1/2 c. shredded Cheddar cheese
10-3/4 oz. can cream of mushroom soup
4 c. corn flake cereal, crushed
1/2 c. butter, melted

SAUSAGE GRAVY & BISCUITS

VICKIE
GOOSEBERRY PATCH

*Enjoy these light and fluffy biscuits topped with hot sausage
gravy any time of the day.*

**2 lbs. ground pork
   sausage
1/2 c. all-purpose flour
4 c. milk
salt and pepper to taste**

1 Brown sausage in a large skillet over medium
heat; drain. Sprinkle flour over sausage, stirring,
stirring until flour is dissolved. Gradually stir in milk
and cook over medium heat until thick and bubbly.
Season with salt and pepper; serve over warm
biscuits.

BISCUITS:
**4 c. self-rising flour
3 T. baking powder
2 T. sugar
7 T. shortening
2 c. buttermilk**

1 Sift together flour, baking powder and sugar; cut
in shortening. Mix in buttermilk with a fork, just until
dough is moistened. Shape dough into a ball and
knead a few times on a lightly floured surface.

2 Roll out to 3/4-inch thickness and cut with a 3-inch
biscuit cutter. Place biscuits on a greased baking
sheet. Bake at 450 degrees for about 15 minutes, or
until golden.

Serves 10 to 12

SOUTHERN CHOCOLATE GRAVY

TINA BUTLER
MESQUITE, TX

My mother used to make chocolate gravy almost every weekend. My brothers, sister and I always got so excited to see the bowl of piping-hot chocolate gravy on the table with a big basket of biscuits! For sweeter gravy, you can increase the amount of sugar to 3/4 cup.

1 Combine sugar, flour and cocoa in a saucepan. Whisk in milk. Bring to a boil over medium heat, then reduce heat, stirring constantly to prevent scorching. When gravy thickens, remove from heat; stir in butter and vanilla. Serve over warm biscuits.

Makes 4 servings

1/2 c. sugar
2 T. all-purpose flour
1 T. baking cocoa
1-1/4 c. milk
1 T. butter
1/2 t. vanilla extract
4 biscuits, split

SWEETIE BANANA OATMEAL

ATHENA COLEGROVE
BIG SPRINGS, TX

My little ones, with Daddy's help, made this for me on Valentine's Day...what a yummy breakfast surprise from my 3 sweeties!

1 Combine oats, milk and water in a slow cooker that has been sprayed with non-stick vegetable spray. Cover and cook on low setting for 6 to 8 hours. Add bananas 10 to 15 minutes before serving.

Serves 4

2 c. long-cooking oats, uncooked
1/2 c. sweetened condensed milk
4 c. water
2 bananas, thinly sliced

CHAPTER TWO

TALL IN THE SADDLE

Soup, Salads & Sandwiches

GET THEM FILLED UP

AND READY TO RIDE WITH

THESE WARM AND

HEARTY SOUPS, FRESH-FROM-

THE-RANCH SALADS AND

PACKED-WITH-GOODNESS

SANDWICHES.

APPLE-WALNUT CHICKEN SALAD

BECKY BUTLER
KELLER, TX

This tasty recipe uses the convenience of a roast chicken from your grocery store's deli...what a great time-saver!

6 c. mixed field greens or baby greens
2 c. deli roast chicken, shredded
1/3 c. crumbled blue cheese
1/4 c. chopped walnuts, toasted
1 Fuji or Gala apple, cored and chopped

1 In a large salad bowl, toss together all ingredients. Drizzle Balsamic Apple Vinaigrette over salad, tossing gently to coat. Serve immediately.

Makes 6 servings

BALSAMIC APPLE VINAIGRETTE:

2 T. frozen apple juice concentrate
1 T. cider vinegar
1 T. white balsamic vinegar
1 t. Dijon mustard
1/4 t. garlic powder
1/3 c. olive oil

1 Whisk together all ingredients in a small bowl. Store any unused portion of the dressing in refrigerator until ready to use.

BAJA SHRIMP QUESADILLAS

JO ANN
GOOSEBERRY PATCH

*These quesadillas are really so easy and so very yummy...
everyone loves them!*

1 Chop shrimp, discarding tails. Mix shrimp, cheese,
mayonnaise, salsa, cumin and peppers; spread one
to 2 tablespoons on one tortilla. Place another tortilla
on top; put on a greased baking sheet. Repeat with
remaining tortillas. Bake at 350 degrees for
15 minutes; remove and cut into small triangles.

Makes about 4 dozen

2-1/2 lbs. shrimp,
  peeled and cleaned
3 c. shredded Cheddar
  cheese
1/2 c. mayonnaise
3/4 c. salsa
1/4 t. ground cumin
1/4 t. cayenne pepper
1/4 t. pepper
12 6-inch flour
  tortillas

CABBAGE PATCH STEW

AMY WOODS
GAINESVILLE, TX

*A creamy, cheesy cabbage stew with a little chile kick! Substitute
plain diced tomatoes if your family prefers milder dishes.*

1 Place ground beef in a large stockpot; sauté until
browned. Drain. Add cabbage and just enough
water to cover. Simmer until cabbage is tender; add
remaining ingredients. Simmer for 20 minutes.

Serves 6 to 8

2 lbs. ground beef
1 head cabbage,
  chopped
2 10-3/4 oz. cans
  cream of mushroom
  soup
2 10-3/4 oz. cans
  Cheddar cheese soup
2 10-oz. cans diced
  tomatoes with green
  chiles

BETTY'S HOT CHEESE TOAST

CONNIE CHAMBERS
COLORADO CITY, TX

This simple recipe has always been a favorite in our family!

1 c. mayonnaise
2 t. Worcestershire
  sauce
1/2 t. ranch salad
  dressing mix
1/4 t. paprika
2 green onions, chopped
2-1/2 oz. pkg. chopped
  almonds
8-oz. pkg. shredded
  Cheddar cheese
2 T. bacon bits
15 bread slices, halved

1 Combine all ingredients except bread slices; mix well. Spread on half-slices of bread; arrange slices on a lightly greased baking sheet. Bake at 400 degrees for 10 minutes, until golden. Serve hot.

Serves 12 to 15

CHICKEN CORN CHOWDER

KATIE FRENCH
PORTLAND, TX

A quick main dish that goes great with a big, buttery piece of cornbread.

1-1/2 c. milk
10-1/2 oz. can chicken
  broth
10-3/4 oz. can cream of
  chicken soup
10-3/4 oz. can cream of
  potato soup
1 to 2 10-oz. cans
  chicken, drained
1/3 c. green onion,
  chopped
11-oz. can sweet corn &
  diced peppers
4-oz. can chopped green
  chiles, drained
8-oz. pkg. shredded
  Cheddar cheese

1 Mix together all ingredients except cheese in a stockpot. Cook over low heat, stirring frequently, for 15 minutes, or until heated through. Add cheese; stir until melted.

Serves 6 to 8

CHEESY CHICKEN & NOODLE SOUP

**CHRISTI PERRY
DENTON, TX**

Spice up this classic by topping it with shredded Pepper Jack cheese.

1 Combine chicken broth, soup and chicken in a large stockpot. Bring to a boil over medium heat, stirring occasionally. Add noodles. Reduce heat to medium-low; simmer until noodles are soft. Stir in milk. Spoon into bowls; sprinkle with cheese if desired.

Serves 6 to 8

> 4 to 6 c. chicken broth
>
> 10-3/4 oz. can Cheddar cheese soup
>
> 2 to 3 c. chicken, cooked and shredded
>
> 8-oz. pkg. fine egg noodles, uncooked
>
> 1 c. milk
>
> Optional: shredded Cheddar cheese

TEXAS RANCH SOUP

**DEBORAH NEUMAN
SAN FELIPE, TX**

So good, this may only make 2 Texas-size servings!

1 Combine all ingredients except garnish in a large stockpot; bring to a boil. Reduce heat and simmer for 15 minutes. Spoon into serving bowls; garnish with crushed tortilla chips and shredded Cheddar cheese.

Serves 6

> 1-1/2 lbs. ground beef, browned and drained
>
> 2 15-oz. cans ranch-style beans
>
> 2 15-oz. cans corn
>
> 2 14-1/2 cans diced tomatoes
>
> 1-1/4 oz. pkg. taco seasoning mix
>
> Garnish: crushed tortilla chips and shredded Cheddar cheese

COUNTRY MINESTRONE SOUP

ERICA CLOPTON
FORT WORTH, TX

This tasty recipe was given to me by my mother-in-law. She is a great cook!

2 T. canola oil
1 c. onion, chopped
1/2 c. celery, sliced
14-1/2 oz. can beef broth
10-3/4 oz. can bean with bacon soup
2-3/4 c. water
1 t. dried basil
1/2 t. salt
1/2 t. pepper
14-1/2 oz. can diced tomatoes
8-oz. pkg. elbow macaroni, uncooked
1 c. cabbage, chopped
1 c. zucchini, cubed
1 c. yellow squash, cubed
1/2 t. beef bouillon granules
2 slices bacon, crisply cooked and diced

1 In a heavy skillet, add canola oil and sauté onion and celery until tender. Stir in broth, soup, water, basil, salt, pepper and tomatoes with juice. Bring to a boil; reduce heat and simmer 10 minutes.

2 Add remaining ingredients except bacon. Simmer for 10 minutes, or until macaroni and vegetables are tender. Garnish with bacon.

Serves 8

ERMA LEE'S CHICKEN SOUP

SHIRLEY WHITE
GATESVILLE, TX

My family still requests this soup at the first sign of any cold weather.

1 Bring broth to a boil in a stockpot over medium heat. Add vegetables; cook until tender, about 10 minutes. Stir in remaining ingredients; simmer over low heat until cheeses melt and soup is heated through, about 15 minutes.

Serves 6 to 8

- 3 14-1/2 oz. cans chicken broth
- 2/3 c. onion, diced
- 2/3 c. carrot, peeled and diced
- 2/3 c. celery, diced
- 2 10-3/4 oz. cans cream of mushroom soup
- 4 boneless, skinless chicken breasts, cooked and chopped
- 8-oz. pkg. pasteurized process cheese spread, cubed
- 1 c. shredded Cheddar cheese
- 1 c. cooked rice

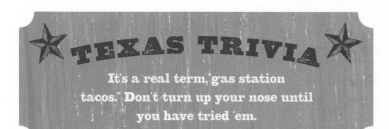

TEXAS TRIVIA

It's a real term, "gas station tacos." Don't turn up your nose until you have tried 'em.

EVELYN'S CUCUMBER SALAD

ALICE JOY RANDALL
NACOGDOCHES, TX

This recipe was given to me by a very dear friend and co-worker.
It was his mother's recipe and is very tasty.

4 ripe tomatoes, chopped
4 cucumbers, peeled and
   chopped
1 onion, chopped
salt and pepper to taste
Italian salad dressing
   to taste

1 Combine vegetables in a bowl; season with salt and pepper. Add desired amount of salad dressing; toss well to mix. Cover and refrigerate overnight before serving.

Makes 6 servings

THE ULTIMATE SHRIMP SANDWICH

KAREN PILCHER
BURLESON, TX

If you like shrimp, you'll really love this sandwich!

3/4 lb. cooked shrimp,
   chopped
1/4 c. green pepper,
   chopped
1/4 c. celery, chopped
1/4 c. cucumber, chopped
1/4 c. tomato, diced
1/4 c. green onion,
   chopped
2 T. mayonnaise
Optional: hot pepper
   sauce to taste
1 c. lettuce, shredded
6 split-top wheat rolls,
   split and lightly
   toasted

1 In a bowl, combine shrimp, vegetables and mayonnaise; toss well. Set aside. Divide lettuce among rolls. Top with shrimp mixture.

Makes 6 servings

TEXAS 2-STEP SANDWICHES

CONNIE HILTY
PEARLAND, TX

This sandwich is so good, it'll have you doing the Texas 2-step!

1 Pour water into a saucepan; stir in vinegar and onion. Bring to a boil; turn off heat and let stand 30 minutes. Drain. Purée beans and cumin in a blender; set side. Stir together mayonnaise, chile and juice in a bowl; spread on 4 slices of bread. Top with bean purée, onion and remaining ingredients; serve open-faced.

Serves 4

1 c. water

1/2 c. white wine vinegar

1 c. red onion, thinly sliced

1 c. canned black beans, drained and rinsed

1/2 t. ground cumin

1/4 c. mayonnaise

1 t. canned chipotle chile, finely chopped

1 T. lime juice

4 slices bread

2/3 c. crumbled feta cheese

1 avocado, peeled, pitted and thinly sliced

2 T. fresh cilantro, chopped

1 tomato, cut into 8 slices

BLUE RIBBON IDEA

A toasty touch for soups! Butter bread slices and cut into shapes using mini cookie cutters. Bake on a baking sheet at 425 degrees until crisp, then garnish filled soup bowls before serving.

FRUIT COMPOTE

VICKIE
GOOSEBERRY PATCH

So simple, so fresh and so beautiful! If you don't want to use bourbon, use local honey and a little more lemon juice. Make the syrup ahead of time and have it ready to toss with the fruit right before serving.

SYRUP:
1 c. water
1/4 c. sugar
3/4 c. fresh mint, chopped
1/4 c. bourbon
1 T. fresh lemon juice

COMPOTE:
1/4 cantaloupe, seeded
1/4 honeydew melon, seeded
1/2 lb. sweet cherries, pitted
2 ripe peaches, pitted and thinly sliced
3 T. fresh mint, thinly sliced
Garnish: fresh mint sprigs

1 To make syrup, combine water and sugar in a medium saucepan over low heat until sugar dissolves. Add mint and boil 5 minutes over medium heat. Let cool completely. Strain into a bowl, pressing firmly on the mint to extract flavor. Mix bourbon and lemon juice into syrup. Cover and refrigerate.

2 Scoop melons with a melon baller. Combine all fruits in a large bowl; add syrup and toss. Refrigerate 30 minutes. Spoon into pretty pedestal glasses and garnish with mint sprigs.

Makes 6 servings

GRANDMOTHER'S RED-HOT SALAD

TRACEE CUMMINS
AMARILLO, TX

My great-grandmother was the perfect hostess. She always wore an apron and rarely sat down at family meals. Everything was always perfect at her table, from the sparkling china to the way the side dishes complemented the main course. She always served this salad at Easter alongside her beautiful baked ham...the spiciness of the salad is a perfect accompaniment to the mild flavor of the ham.

1 Add desired amount of candies to boiling water, depending on how spicy you want your salad to be. Stir until candies are melted; strain out any unmelted bits. Stir in dry gelatin mix until dissolved; add applesauce and mix well. Pour into a serving dish; chill until set.

1/2 to 1 c. red cinnamon candies
1 c. boiling water
3-oz. pkg. cherry gelatin mix
1 c. applesauce

Serves 6

PORK & SAUERKRAUT STEW

KAREN PILCHER
BURLESONL, TX

This stew conjures up warm and comforting memories of growing up in the Midwest. It has a really good flavor and the meat is so tender.

1 Spread sauerkraut in a large Dutch oven; add pork, cabbage and onion. Set aside.

2 In a medium bowl, stir together remaining ingredients except potatoes; add to Dutch oven. Bring to a boil over medium high heat; reduce heat and simmer for 2-1/2 hours, stirring occasionally. Add potatoes; cover and continue to simmer until potatoes are tender, about one hour.

2 14-oz. cans sauerkraut, drained
3 lbs. country-style pork ribs
4 c. cabbage, shredded
2 c. onion, coarsely chopped
2 T. brown sugar, packed
2 T. Worcestershire sauce
1-1/2 oz. pkg. onion soup mix
1 t. caraway seed
1-1/2 c. water
1-1/2 lbs. redskin potatoes, peeled and sliced

Serves 6

YANKEE CHILI

KATHLEEN PETERS
ARLINGTON, TX

I learned this recipe from my grandmother. Originally from Poland, she came to America and settled in Batavia, New York. A friend of hers there taught her to make this chili and it is truly my favorite. When a church I was attending in Dallas had a chili cook-off, everyone said my Yankee Chili didn't stand a chance...but it won!

2 lbs. ground beef
1 onion, chopped
1 green pepper, chopped
28-oz. can whole
  tomatoes
15-1/2 oz. can kidney
  beans
10-3/4 oz. can tomato
  soup
2 T. chili powder
2 t. dried cumin
2 t. paprika
Garnish: shredded
  cheese, chopped onions,
  crackers, bread &
  butter

1 In a Dutch oven over medium-high heat, brown beef with onion and green pepper for 10 to 12 minutes. Drain; add tomatoes with juice, beans with juice, soup and seasonings. Stir to combine and bring to a boil. Turn heat to medium-low and simmer for one to 2 hours. Stir occasionally, breaking up whole tomatoes with the back of your spoon. Garnish as desired.

Serves 6

★ TEXAS TRIVIA ★

When it comes to Texas chili, don't fight it. **NO WAY, NO BEANS** for most Texans.

ITALIAN MEATLOAF SANDWICHES

JO ANN
GOOSEBERRY PATCH

This sandwich is great to come in and eat after you have been working outside and feel like a really good, filling meal.

1 Cut bread into fourths; cut quarters in half horizontally. Place bread quarters, cut-side up, on a baking sheet. Top each bread bottom with one meatloaf slice, 2 tablespoons marinara sauce and 1/4 cup cheese. Top each bread top with 2 tablespoons marinara sauce and 1/4 cup cheese; sprinkle with Italian seasoning.

2 Bake at 375 degrees for 10 to 15 minutes, or until cheese melts and meat is thoroughly heated. Top bread bottoms with bread tops and serve sandwiches immediately.

Makes 4 servings

> 14-oz. loaf French bread
> 4 (1-inch-thick) slices cold meatloaf
> 1 c. marinara or spaghetti sauce
> 8-oz. pkg. shredded Italian-blend cheese
> 1/4 t. Italian seasoning

HAM & OLIVE ROLL-UPS

LISA HEROLD
ABILENE, TX

This is a yummy snack for anyone on the go! A neighbor gave me this recipe during the holidays.

1 Pat ham slices dry with a paper towel. Spread cream cheese over one side of each ham slice. Sprinkle with pimentos, if desired. Roll up ham slice jelly-roll style; slice into one-inch thick pieces. Fasten each roll with a toothpick topped with an olive. Serve immediately or refrigerate until serving time.

Serves 4 to 6

> 1 lb. deli sliced ham
> 2 8-oz. pkgs. cream cheese, softened
> Optional: 1 T. pimentos, minced
> 4-1/2 oz. can whole black olives, drained

JANIE'S 5-CAN SOUP

JULIE BAYLESS
BURLESON, TX

I got this recipe from my friend Janie, who had big, hungry boys to feed. It is so easy and yummy. I try to keep the ingredients in my pantry so it's ready to make on busy days. Great with tortilla chips and Cheddar cheese on top too.

15-oz. can ranch-style beans
14-3/4 oz. can creamed corn
10-3/4 oz. can chicken & rice soup
10-oz. can diced tomatoes with green chiles
13-oz. can cooked chicken

1 Combine all ingredients in a large saucepan; do not drain. Simmer over medium-low heat until bubbly and heated through.

Makes 8 servings

PIG-IN-A-POKE HAM SOUP

SONIA HAWKINS
AMARILLO, TX

A tasty use for the bone left over from a holiday ham! Or get a smoked ham hock at the butcher's counter.

4 14-1/2 oz. cans green beans
1 meaty ham bone
4 potatoes, peeled and quartered
1 onion, sliced
pepper to taste

1 In a slow cooker, combine undrained green beans and remaining ingredients. Cover and cook on high setting for one hour. Reduce to low setting; cover and cook for 6 to 7 hours, until the meat falls off the bone. Remove ham bone; dice meat and return to slow cooker.

Makes 10 servings

KRISTIN'S PEASANT STEW

KRISTIN STONE
LITTLE ELM, TX

I call this Peasant Stew because it's so easy on the budget! It is also easy to make and everyone always loves it. I serve it with warm whole-grain bread and Cheddar cheese. Yum!

1 Sprinkle eggplant slices with salt on both sides. Let stand for 30 minutes; rinse well, drain and chop. Heat oil in a large stockpot over medium heat. Add eggplant, zucchini and seasonings; sauté until vegetables are crisp-tender.

2 Add broth; bring to a boil. Stir in macaroni. Reduce heat and simmer for 10 minutes, or until macaroni is tender. Stir in beans; heat through.

Makes 6 servings

1 eggplant, peeled and thickly sliced

1/4 t. salt

2 T. olive oil

2 zucchini, halved lengthwise and thickly sliced

2 t. dried basil

1/8 t. garlic salt

4 c. chicken broth

1/2 c. elbow macaroni, uncooked

15-oz. can kidney beans, drained and rinsed

KITCHEN TIP

Drain and rinse canned beans before using...you'll be washing away any "tinny" taste. The added bonus is that you'll reduce the sodium content as well.

LYNDA'S SALMON BURGERS

LYNDA MCCORMICK
BURKBURNETT, TX

My entire family loves these salmon burgers. I usually serve them with fresh berries or pineapple.

1 lb. salmon fillet, skin removed and chopped

1/2 c. red onion, finely chopped

1/4 c. fresh basil, thinly sliced

1/4 t. salt

1/4 t. pepper

1 egg white

1 T. sriracha hot chili sauce

Optional: 1/4 c. panko bread crumbs

8 slices whole-grain bread, toasted and cut in half

Garnish: lettuce leaves, tomato slices

1 In a large bowl, combine salmon, onion, basil and seasonings; mix gently. In a small bowl, whisk together egg white and chili sauce. Add to salmon mixture and stir well to combine. If mixture is too soft, stir in bread crumbs if desired. Form mixture into 8 patties, 1/4-inch thick.

2 Heat a large non-stick skillet over medium-high heat. Coat pan with non-stick vegetable spray. Add patties to skillet; cook for about 2 to 3 minutes per side. Place patties sandwich-style on toasted wheat bread. Garnish with lettuce and tomato if desired.

Makes 8 servings

LISA'S CHICKEN TORTILLA SOUP

LISA JOHNSON
HALLSVILLE, TX

My family loves this on a cold winter night. I like to garnish mine with fresh cilantro, but my family likes lots of shredded cheese on theirs. However you like it garnished, it is wonderful!

1 Combine broth and tomatoes with chiles in a large stockpot over medium heat. Stir in corn and beans; bring to a boil. Reduce heat to low and simmer 5 minutes, stirring frequently. Add chicken and heat through. Garnish bowls of soup as desired.

Makes 8 servings

4 14-1/2 oz. cans chicken broth

4 10-oz. cans diced tomatoes with green chiles

1 c. canned or frozen corn

30-oz. can refried beans

4-3/4 c. cooked chicken, shredded

Garnish: shredded Mexican-blend cheese, corn chips or tortilla strips, chopped fresh cilantro

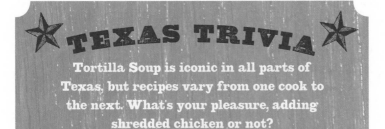

TEXAS TRIVIA

Tortilla Soup is iconic in all parts of Texas, but recipes vary from one cook to the next. What's your pleasure, adding shredded chicken or not?

MUFFULETTA SANDWICH

**FAITH ROBINSON
HOUSTON, TX**

This New Orleans-inspired sandwich is similar to an Italian hero-style sandwich made with a variety of meats and cheeses layered on a round loaf. But what makes it distinctively a muffuletta is the olive salad.

3/4 c. green olives, chopped

3/4 c. black olives, chopped

1 clove garlic, minced

1/3 c. chopped pimentos

1/4 c. fresh parsley, chopped

3/4 t. dried oregano

1/4 t. pepper

1/3 c. plus 1 T. olive oil, divided

1 round loaf Italian bread

1/2 lb. sliced honey ham

1/2 lb. sliced deli turkey

1/4 lb. sliced Muenster cheese

Optional: mayonnaise-type salad dressing

8 to 10 dill pickle slices

1 Mix olives, garlic, pimentos, parsley, seasonings and 1/3 cup oil in a small bowl; set aside. Cut loaf in half horizontally and hollow out the center. Brush cut side of bottom half with remaining oil; layer ham, turkey and cheese slices on top. Spread salad dressing between the layers, if desired. Top with pickle slices. Fill top half of loaf with the olive mixture; place bottom loaf on top and invert.

2 Wrap tightly in plastic wrap and chill overnight. Let stand until loaf comes to room temperature; cut into wedges.

Serves 6 to 8

O'BRIEN-STYLE POTATO SOUP

BRENDA HUGHES
HOUSTON, TX

I make this a day ahead...it's always best the second day. So easy with very few ingredients. Frozen hashbrowns that already include the peppers and onions save chopping time!

1 Combine potatoes, broth and gravy mix in a stockpot over medium heat. Bring to a boil, stirring often. Reduce heat to low; simmer for 20 minutes. Stir in half-and-half. Simmer over low heat for 10 to 15 minutes, but do not boil. Soup will gradually thicken. Serve immediately, or cover, refrigerate overnight and rewarm to serve the next day.

Makes 6 servings

28-oz. pkg. frozen diced hashbrowns with onions and peppers
3 14-oz. cans chicken broth
2-3/4 oz. pkg. peppered white gravy mix
1/2 c. half-and-half

TURKEY & BERRY SANDWICHES

KIM HINSHAW
AUSTIN, TX

I served these sandwiches to friends while we were vacationing at the beach. Everyone raved about them and requested the recipe!

1 Layer lettuce, cheese, turkey and strawberries on 2 slices of bread. Combine cream cheese and pecans. Spread over remaining bread slices; close sandwiches.

Serves 2

2 lettuce leaves
2 slices Swiss cheese
1/4 lb. thinly sliced low-sodium deli turkey
4 strawberries, hulled and sliced
4 slices thinly-sliced whole-wheat bread
2 T. whipped cream cheese spread
2 t. pecans, finely chopped

PANTRY TOMATO SOUP

PATRICIA RODGERS
KATY, TX

One cold and blustery day, I wasn't planning to do any shopping for lunch. So I decided to raid the pantry and make something warm and delicious. It was an experiment that turned out great! Serve with grilled cheese, crackers or croutons.

2 15-oz. cans tomato sauce or crushed tomatoes
1/2 t. baking soda
2 12-oz. cans evaporated milk
3 dashes hot pepper sauce
1/4 t. pepper
1/4 t. Greek seasoning
Optional: dried basil to taste

1 Add tomato sauce to a saucepan over medium heat; sprinkle with baking soda and stir. Add remaining ingredients; mix well. Cook, stirring occasionally, until hot and bubbly.

Serves 6 to 8

EASY GOULASH

KIMBERLY BASORE
GARLAND, TX

Replace the kidney beans with navy beans, if you prefer.

1 lb. ground beef
1/4 c. onion, chopped
14-1/2 oz. can stewed tomatoes
3/4 c. water
salt and pepper to taste
2 c. elbow macaroni, uncooked
15-1/4 oz. can corn, drained
15-oz. can kidney beans, drained and rinsed
16-oz. pkg. pasteurized process cheese spread, cubed

1 Brown beef and onion in a large stockpot over medium heat; drain. Add tomatoes with juice and water; sprinkle with salt and pepper to taste.

2 Add macaroni and simmer for 8 to 10 minutes, until macaroni is tender, adding more water if necessary. Add corn, beans and cheese; heat until cheese is melted.

Serves 4 to 6

ROASTED VEGGIE PANINI

LYNDA MCCORMICK
BURKBURNETT, TX

If you don't have a panini press, place the sandwiches in a hot skillet and gently press them with a smaller heavy pan; cook over medium-low heat until the cheese melts.

1 Combine zucchini, squash and mushrooms in a large bowl; toss with one teaspoon olive oil and vinegar. Grill, covered, over medium-high heat,15 to 20 minutes, turning occasionally; set aside.

2 Heat one teaspoon olive oil in a skillet over medium heat. Add onion and cook 15 minutes or until caramelized, stirring often; set aside.

3 Spread tops and bottoms of bread slices with olive tapénade; layer pepper rings, spinach, tomatoes and cheese evenly on half the bread slices and top with remaining bread slices. Preheat panini press according to manufacturer's instructions. Place sandwiches in press (in batches, if necessary); cook 3 to 4 minutes, or until cheese melts and bread is toasted.

Note: Look for olive tapenade in the deli section of larger supermarkets.

Serves 4

2 zucchini, sliced
1 yellow squash, sliced
6 oz. portobello mushroom caps, sliced
2 t. olive oil, divided
1 t. balsamic vinegar
1 sweet onion, thinly sliced
1 loaf sourdough bread, sliced
1/4 c. olive tapénade
1 red pepper, sliced into rings
1 green pepper, sliced into rings
1 yellow pepper, sliced into rings
1 c. spinach leaves
2 roma tomatoes, sliced
4 slices provolone cheese

SPICY CHICKEN SOUP

STEPHANIE JENKINS
MCKINNEY, TX

This zesty, fresh soup is my husband's absolute favorite! When he was living in Guatemala as a missionary, I taught him how to make it, and he made it every week. Now, a bowl of this soup brings back memories for him.

1 lb. chicken breasts
  and/or thighs
1 onion, chopped
1 jalapeño pepper,
  seeded and minced
4 cloves garlic, minced
4 carrots, peeled and
  thinly sliced
8 c. water
1/4 t. salt
1/4 t. pepper
3/4 c. long-cooking
  brown rice, uncooked
Garnish: lime wedges,
  avocado slices,
  shredded Monterey
  Jack cheese

1 In a large soup pot over medium-high heat, combine all ingredients except rice and garnish. Bring to a boil; reduce heat to medium-low. Simmer, partially covered, for 45 minutes, or until chicken juices run clear.

2 Remove chicken and set aside to cool, reserving broth in soup pot. Return broth to a boil; stir in rice. Reduce heat to low and simmer, covered, for 45 minutes, or until rice is tender.

3 Meanwhile, shred chicken, discarding skin and bones. When rice is tender, return chicken to the pot and heat through. Serve soup in large bowls, garnished with a squeeze of lime juice, a few slices of avocado and a sprinkling of cheese.

Makes 6 servings

SPICY POTATO-BEEF SOUP

SUZAN MECHLING
ROUND ROCK, TX

*I was born and raised in Ohio before we moved to Texas several years
ago. This was such a quick & easy soup to make on a cold day.*

1 In a Dutch oven or large kettle, brown beef over
medium heat; drain. Add remaining ingredients; bring
to a boil. Reduce heat to medium-low. Simmer for
one hour, stirring occasionally, or until potatoes are
tender and soup has thickened.

Makes 6 to 8 servings

1 lb. ground beef

4 c. potatoes, peeled and
cubed

1/2 c. onion, chopped

3 8-oz. cans tomato
sauce

4 c. water

1/2 to 1 t. hot pepper
sauce

2 t. salt

1-1/2 t. pepper

DIRTY GREEK RICE

BEA GARCIA
SAN ANTONIO, TX

*This savory rice goes well with chicken, beef and fish...in other
words, with just about anything! It's been a family favorite
for twenty-five years.*

1 Heat reserved drippings in a skillet over medium
heat. Add rice and sauté, cooking and stirring
until golden. Add remaining ingredients including
crumbled bacon. Bring to a boil; reduce heat to low.
Cover and simmer for 35 to 40 minutes, until rice is
tender. Fluff with a fork before serving.

Serves 6

4 slices bacon, crisply
cooked and crumbled,
drippings reserved

1-1/2 c. long-cooking rice,
uncooked

6 green onions, chopped

2 cloves garlic, minced

2-1/4 oz. can sliced black
olives, drained

1 t. Greek seasoning

1 t. salt

3 c. water

STRAWBERRY-MELON SALAD

SANDRA BINS
GEORGETOWN, TX

I love to make this dish during strawberry season. It is super easy to make and everyone always loves it...so refreshing!

1 cantaloupe, peeled, seeded and cubed
1 honeydew or Crenshaw melon, peeled, seeded and cubed
1 c. celery, chopped
Banana-Yogurt Dressing
1 c. strawberries, hulled and quartered

1 Combine melon cubes and celery in a large bowl. Drizzle with Banana-Yogurt Dressing; toss to mix. Top with strawberries and serve immediately.

Makes 8 servings

BANANA-YOGURT DRESSING:

1/2 c. plain yogurt
1/4 c. orange juice
1 banana, sliced

1 Place all ingredients in a blender or food processor. Cover and blend until puréed.

THE BEST-EVER POTATO SALAD

SHELLYE MCDANIEL
TEXARKANA, TX

A homestyle potato salad that's just plain good! I cook the potatoes and eggs ahead of time and keep refrigerated until time to put the salad together. So yummy!

1 Combine all ingredients in a large serving bowl; mix well. Cover and refrigerate until serving.

Serves 6 to 8

4 c. potatoes, peeled, cubed and boiled

1 c. mayonnaise

4 eggs, hard-boiled, peeled and chopped

1-1/2 c. celery, chopped

1/4 c. radishes chopped

1/2 c. green onions, chopped

2 T. fresh parsley, chopped

1 T. cider vinegar

2 t. mustard

1-1/2 t. salt

1 t. pepper

1/2 t. celery seed

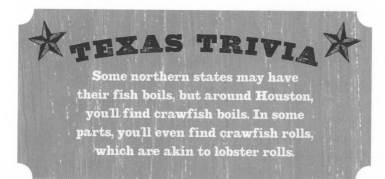

TEXAS TRIVIA

Some northern states may have their fish boils, but around Houston, you'll find crawfish boils. In some parts, you'll even find crawfish rolls, which are akin to lobster rolls.

COUNTRY PEA & BEAN SALAD

SANDY BRUMMETT
HENDERSON, TX

My husband loves this salad...there are lots of loving memories in it!
It was served every Thanksgiving at my parents. Now I have
the salad bowl that Mother used to fix it in and I still use it every
Thanksgiving for this salad.

15-oz. can shoepeg corn,
  drained
15-1/4 oz. can peas,
  drained
14-1/2 oz. can French-
  style green beans,
  drained
2-oz. jar chopped
  pimentos, drained
1 green pepper, chopped
1 onion, chopped
3 stalks celery, chopped

1 Combine all ingredients in a large bowl; toss to mix. Cover and chill overnight before serving.

Serves 12

SUMMERTIME FETA & TOMATOES

REBECCA PICKETT
HOUSTON, TX

We love to change up the spices and vinegars in this recipe each
time we make it. If you eat all the tomatoes and still have dressing
left, dip some crusty bread in it!

7 roma tomatoes,
  chopped
4-oz. pkg. crumbled feta
  cheese
1/4 c. olive oil
1/2 c. red wine vinegar
2 t. Italian seasoning
1/4 t. seasoned salt

1 Combine all ingredients; toss to blend. Refrigerate for 30 minutes to allow flavors to blend.

Serves 8

EASY TACO SOUP

CARIE VANCLEAVE
ABILENE, TX

One day I was so hungry for soup. I found some canned beans, tomatoes and corn in the pantry, added a few other ingredients and made a fantastic soup...my family loves it! Garnish it with shredded cheese and crushed tortilla chips.

1 In a large stockpot over medium heat, cook ground beef until browned; drain. Stir in remaining ingredients.

2 Reduce heat and simmer until squash and zucchini are tender, about 15 minutes.

Serves 8

1 lb. ground beef
14-1/2 oz. can beef broth
16-oz. can pinto beans
16-oz. can black beans
15-1/4 oz. can corn
10-oz. can diced
  tomatoes with chiles
1 yellow squash, chopped
1 zucchini, chopped
2 c. water
1-1/4 oz. pkg. taco
  seasoning mix
1-oz. pkg. ranch salad
  dressing mix
2 T. fresh cilantro,
  chopped
salt and pepper to taste

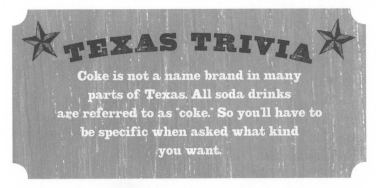

★ TEXAS TRIVIA ★

Coke is not a name brand in many parts of Texas. All soda drinks are referred to as "coke." So you'll have to be specific when asked what kind you want.

RIO GRANDE GREEN PORK CHILI

**DEBBY HEATWOLE
CANADIAN, TX**

*Makes a wonderful buffet dish served with warm flour tortillas, or
spoon over potato-filled burritos…yum!*

3 lbs. boneless pork loin,
  cubed
1 clove garlic, minced
3 T. olive oil
1/3 c. all-purpose flour
2 14-1/2-oz. cans low-
  sodium beef broth
32-oz. can tomato juice
14-1/2 oz. can crushed
  tomatoes
7-oz. can diced green
  chiles
1/4 c. chopped jalapeño
  peppers
1/3 c. dried parsley
1/4 c. lemon juice
2 t. ground cumin
1 t. sugar
1/4 t. ground cloves

1 In a heavy skillet over medium heat, sauté pork
and garlic in oil. Add flour, stirring until thoroughly
mixed.

2 Place browned pork in a 6-quart slow cooker.
Add remaining ingredients; cover and cook on low
setting for 6 to 8 hours, until pork is tender. Garnish
as desired.

Makes 14 servings

FOOD FOR THOUGHT

**What good fortune to grow up
in a home where there are grandparents
nearby.** — Suzanne LaFollette

CHEESEBURGER SOUP

LACY MAYFIELD
EARTH, TX

All the ingredients of your favorite cheeseburger are included in this chunky soup.

1 Combine first 8 ingredients in a large saucepan; bring to a boil over medium heat. Reduce heat and simmer until potatoes are tender. Stir in beef and 2 cups milk.

2 Whisk together flour and remaining milk in a small bowl until smooth; gradually whisk into soup. Bring to a boil; cook 2 minutes or until thick and bubbly, stirring constantly. Reduce heat; add cheese and stir until melted. Add cayenne pepper, if desired. Garnish with bacon.

Serves 6 to 8

2 c. potatoes, peeled and cubed

2 carrots, peeled and grated

1 onion, chopped

1 jalapeño pepper, seeded and chopped

1 clove garlic, minced

1-1/2 c. water

1 T. beef bouillon granules

1/2 t. salt

1 lb. ground beef, browned and drained

2-1/2 c. milk, divided

3 T. all-purpose flour

8-oz. pkg. pasteurized process cheese spread, cubed

Optional: 1/4 to 1 t. cayenne pepper

Garnish: 1/2 lb. bacon, crisply cooked and crumbled

CHAPTER THREE

MIGHTY GOOD
Mains &
Sides

FILL THEM UP WITH A

STICK-TO-THE-RIBS MEAL THAT

IS FULL OF FLAVOR AND SETS

THE STAGE FOR A "DON'T MESS

WITH TEXAS" DAY.

5-CAN MEXICAN MEAL

BRENDA HUGHES
HOUSTON, TX

In a hurry? I opened five cans from my pantry and made the best one-pot meal ever!

15-oz. can beef tamales, unwrapped and cut into 1-inch pieces

16-oz. can light red kidney beans

16-oz. can pinto beans

11-oz. can sweet corn and diced peppers

10-oz. can diced tomatoes with green chiles

1 Combine all ingredients in a large saucepan without draining cans. Cook over medium heat, stirring occasionally, until hot and bubbly.

Makes 6 servings

ZIPPY SHREDDED PORK

JESSICA SANCHEZ
HOUSTON, TX

Sometimes I top these with a little bit of coleslaw. So good!

2 to 3-lb. boneless pork loin roast

salt and pepper to taste

16-oz. jar salsa

Optional: hot pepper sauce, chopped green chiles

6 hard rolls, split

1 Place roast in a slow cooker; sprinkle with salt and pepper. Pour salsa over roast; add hot sauce or chiles for extra heat, if desired. Cover and cook on low setting for 8 to 10 hours, until meat shreds easily. Stir meat to shred completely and serve on rolls.

Makes 6 servings

BLACK-EYED PEA GUMBO

RONDA WOODALL
FRUITVALE, TX

We love this flavorful meatless soup in winter with hot cornbread or cheese biscuits and a crisp tossed salad.

1 Heat oil in a saucepan over medium heat. Add onion, green pepper and celery; cook until tender. Stir in chicken broth; add uncooked rice, garlic and undrained peas and tomatoes. Bring to a boil.

2 Reduce heat to low; simmer 45 minutes or until rice is tender, stirring occasionally and adding a little water if soup gets too thick.

Makes 8 servings

1 T. olive oil

3/4 c. onion, chopped

3/4 c. green pepper, chopped

5 stalks celery, chopped

2 c. chicken broth

1 c. long-cooking brown rice, uncooked

2 cloves garlic, chopped

4 15-oz. cans black-eyed peas

14-1/2 oz. can diced tomatoes

10-oz. can diced tomatoes with green chiles

FLAVOR BOOSTER

If you want to add a little more protein and some kick to a veggie soup, add some slices of cooked link sausage to the mix. Yummy!

BASIL CHICKEN & TORTELLINI

KRISTIN STONE
LITTLE ELM, TX

*This scrumptious dish evolved from a recipe my mother used to make.
We love it...I hope your family will too!*

2-1/2 c. cheese tortellini,
  uncooked
14-oz. pkg. frozen
  broccoli flowerets
3 boneless, skinless
  chicken breasts, cubed
1 t. garlic, minced
1/2 c. basil pesto sauce
1/4 c. chicken broth
2 T. lemon juice
2 T. water
1 T. plus 2 t. fresh basil,
  chopped
Optional: fresh basil
  sprigs

1 Cook pasta according to package directions, adding broccoli along with pasta; drain. Meanwhile, spray a large non-stick skillet with non-stick vegetable spray. Over medium-high heat, cook chicken with garlic for about 2 minutes, until chicken is golden on all sides. Add remaining ingredients except basil sprigs to skillet, stirring to mix. Reduce heat to medium-low.

2 Cover and simmer for 6 to 8 minutes, stirring occasionally, until chicken juices run clear. To serve, spoon chicken mixture over pasta and broccoli. Garnish with basil sprigs, if desired.

Makes 6 servings

TEXAS TRIVIA

Discussing Texas foods requires
a new language. There are flautas
(like rolled tacos), also called taquitos;
chalupas, like a big nacho and also called
tostadas, along with gorditas, a thick,
stuffed pocket. Don't forget empanadas,
like Mexican turnovers, which can have
sweet or savory fillings.

BBQ PORK RIBS

DIANE AXTELL
MARBLE FALLS, TX

When you live in Texas you need a great BBQ Ribs recipe. This is the one we like. Change up the sauce to fit your taste.

1 Bring water to a boil in a large stockpot over high heat. Add ribs, onion, salt and pepper. Reduce heat; cover and simmer for 1-1/2 hours. Remove ribs from pot; drain. Grill ribs for 10 minutes on each side, brushing frequently with BBQ Sauce, until tender.

3 qts. water
4 lbs. pork ribs, cut into
  serving-size portions
1 red onion, quartered
1 t. salt
1/2 t. pepper

1 Combine all ingredients in a small saucepan. Simmer over low heat for one hour, stirring frequently.

Serves 6

BBQ SAUCE:
1/2 c. vinegar
1 T. lemon juice
1/2 c. chili sauce
1/4 c. Worcestershire
  sauce
2 T. onion, chopped
1/2 c. honey
1/2 t. dry mustard
1/8 t. garlic powder
1/8 t. cayenne pepper
1/4 t. red pepper flakes

BEST BEEF BRISKET

LYNDA MCCORMICK
BURKBURNETT, TX

This brisket is fork-tender and delicious.

1 t. garlic salt
1 t. garlic powder
1-3/4 t. kosher salt
2 t. pepper
2 T. Worcestershire sauce
5 to 6-lb. beef brisket, trimmed
1/3 c. sugar
1 c. barbecue sauce
1 c. Russian salad dressing

1 Combine first 5 ingredients; rub into beef. Tightly wrap beef in heavy-duty aluminum foil; place in an ungreased 13"x9" baking pan. Bake at 300 degrees for 5 hours. Carefully remove foil from beef; set beef aside.

2 Measure one cup of broth; discard any remaining broth. Return brisket to baking pan. Mix together one cup broth, sugar, barbecue sauce and salad dressing; pour over brisket. Bake, covered, at 325 degrees for 30 minutes. Uncover and bake 30 more minutes. Serve with sauce.

Serves 10 to 12

BRATS, TATERS & APPLES

DIANE COHEN
THE WOODLANDS, TX

The taste combination of bratwurst, potatoes and apples is something special indeed. It may sound strange, but one bite and you'll be a believer.

5 to 6 bratwurst pork sausage links, sliced
5 potatoes, peeled and cubed
27-oz. pkg. sauerkraut, drained and rinsed
1 tart apple, cored and chopped
1 onion, chopped
1/4 c. brown sugar, packed

1 In a skillet over medium heat, brown bratwurst on all sides. Combine remaining ingredients in a slow cooker. Stir in bratwurst and pan drippings; cover and cook on high setting for 4 to 6 hours, until potatoes and apples are tender.

Serves 6

ALL-PASTA SAUCE

VICKI
GOOSEBERRY PATCH

One taste of this homemade pasta sauce, and you won't be tempted to use the store-bought sauce again! Use in place of tomato or spaghetti sauce all year long.

1 Process tomatoes, green peppers and onions in batches in a blender; add to a large stockpot. Bring to a boil; boil gently for one hour. Stir in tomato paste and next 8 ingredients; boil one more hour. Remove and discard bay leaves.

2 Spoon into hot sterilized jars, leaving 1/2-inch headspace. Add one tablespoon balsamic vinegar to each jar. Remove air bubbles; wipe jar rims. Cover at once with metal lids and screw on bands. Process in a boiling water bath 20 minutes; set jars on a towel to cool.

Makes 4 jars

11 lbs. tomatoes, chopped

2 green peppers, chopped

1-1/2 lbs. onions, chopped

24-oz. can tomato paste

1 c. oil

3/4 c. sugar

1/4 c. canning salt

2 cloves garlic, chopped

2 bay leaves

1-1/2 T. dried basil

1 T. dried parsley

1/2 T. dried oregano

4 (1-qt.) canning jars and lids, sterilized

1/4 c. balsamic vinegar, divided

STEAK & SPINACH PINWHEELS

VICKIE
GOOSEBERRY PATCH

Serve a green salad with this and you will have a complete meal!

1 to 1-1/4 lb. beef flank steak or top round steak, halved lengthwise

3/4 t. lemon-pepper seasoning

1/4 t. salt

8 slices bacon, partially cooked

10-oz. pkg. frozen chopped spinach, thawed and drained

2 T. fine, dry bread crumbs

1/2 t. dried thyme

1 If you're using wooden skewers, be sure to soak them first in water for about 30 minutes to prevent any flare-ups on the grill.

2 With a sharp knife, score both pieces of steak in a diamond pattern with cuts one inch apart. Repeat on other side. Place one piece of steak between 2 lengths of heavy-duty plastic wrap; pound lightly into a 10"x6" rectangle. Repeat with second piece. Blend seasoning and salt; sprinkle each steak evenly with half of seasoning mixture. Arrange 4 slices of bacon lengthwise on each steak; set aside.

3 Combine spinach, bread crumbs and thyme in a bowl; spread half of spinach mixture over each steak. Starting at a short end, roll up each steak. Place toothpicks at one-inch intervals on rolled-up steaks to form 6 one-inch pinwheels from each steak. Slice between toothpicks. Slide 2 pinwheels carefully onto each of 6 skewers. Preheat grill to medium-high heat. Grill pinwheels about 6 to 7 minutes, or to desired degree of doneness.

Serves 6

ENCHILADA CASSEROLE

KATIE FRENCH
PORTLAND, TX

This was one of the first dishes I learned to make as a newlywed. My husband said he'd like to kiss the person who taught it to me.

1 Combine ground beef, sauce and soups in a large bowl. Stir until well mixed. In a greased 13"x9" baking pan, layer half of the tortillas, half of the beef mixture and half of the cheese. Repeat layers. Bake, uncovered at 350 degrees for 30 minutes.

Serves 6 to 10

1-1/2 lbs. ground beef, browned and drained

14-oz. can enchilada sauce

10-3/4 oz. can cream of mushroom soup

10-3/4 oz. can cream of chicken soup

10 corn tortillas, torn

8-oz. pkg. shredded Cheddar cheese

KITCHEN TIP

Colorful, fresh veggies are always welcome at parties and easy to prepare in advance. Cut them into bite-size slices, flowerets or cubes and tuck away in plastic zipping bags until needed . . .what a time-saver!

CAYENNE FRIED CHICKEN

VICKIE
GOOSEBERRY PATCH

*Warm up with this hot & spicy version of classic fried chicken...
we guarantee you'll come back for seconds after your mouth
cools off!*

**4 boneless, skinless
  chicken breasts**

2-1/2 c. milk

**2 T. plus 4 drops hot
  pepper sauce**

1 t. salt

**3/4 c. all-purpose flour,
  divided**

3/4 c. butter, melted

6 T. oil

1/2 t. garlic powder

1 t. fresh chives, chopped

salt and pepper to taste

1 Place chicken in a deep bowl. Cover with milk;
add 2 tablespoons hot sauce and salt. Let stand for
one hour.

2 Remove chicken and coat with 6 tablespoons
flour; set milk mixture aside. Heat 1/3 cup butter and
oil in a large skillet. Cook chicken in butter mixture
until browned on both sides and no longer pink in
the middle; set aside.

3 Drain skillet, reserving 3 tablespoons drippings
in skillet. Add remaining butter and flour; stir until
browned. Pour reserved milk into skillet. Add garlic
powder, chives, remaining hot sauce, salt and
pepper to taste. Bring to a boil; cook and stir until
slightly thickened, about 10 minutes. Spoon sauce
over chicken before serving.

Serves 4

CAJUN CORN MAQUE CHOUX

BECKY BUTLER
KELLER, TX

Maque Choux (pronounced "mock shoe") is a common side dish in the deep south. I grew up eating it with pan-fried pork chops, ham, fried chicken and smothered steak. It is very commonly made using leftover boiled corn from a crawfish boil, which makes it extra spicy! When using frozen corn, I have even added a few drops of liquid Cajun boil seasoning to the dish to duplicate the flavor. If you can't find andouille sausage locally, you can substitute any smoked meat, such as ham or even bacon.

1 Sauté sausage in a large skillet over medium heat for 6 minutes. Remove sausage from pan, reserving drippings in pan. Add enough butter to make 2 tablespoons fat in skillet. Add onion and peppers; cook over medium heat, about 8 minutes. Add corn, tomatoes and sausage; stir well.

2 Cook, stirring often, for 15 minutes. Stir in green onions and Cajun seasoning; cook another 3 to 5 minutes.

Makes 6 to 8 servings

1/4 lb. andouille smoked pork sausage, diced
1 to 2 T. butter
1/2 c. onion, diced
1/4 c. green pepper, diced
1 jalapeño pepper, minced and seeded
3 ears sweet corn, kernels cut off, or 3 c. frozen corn, thawed
1 to 2 tomatoes, diced
1/4 c. green onions, chopped
1/2 t. Cajun seasoning, or to taste

CHEESY HOMINY

**PATTI WAFFORD
MOUNT VERNON, TX**

*My family always requests this as a side when we're having my
mom's homemade hot tamales. It's ooey-gooey goodness and is
so simple to make!*

**2 15-1/2 oz. cans yellow
hominy, drained
10-3/4 oz. can cream of
celery soup
8-oz. pkg. Mexican or
regular pasteurized
process cheese, cubed**

1 Combine hominy, soup and cheese in a
microwave-safe dish. Microwave on high until
cheese is melted, stirring every few minutes.

Makes 6 to 8 servings

SWEET-AND-SOUR PORK

**JANICE DORSEY
SAN ANTONIO, TX**

*No need for take-out when this popular Asian dish is ready and
waiting in the slow cooker.*

**1 onion, chopped
1-1/2 lbs. pork loin, cubed
14-oz. can chicken broth
10-oz. bottle sweet-and-
sour sauce
15-1/4 oz. can pineapple
chunks, drained
2 green peppers, chopped
1 c. long-cooking rice,
uncooked**

1 Place onion in a 5-quart slow cooker; top with
pork, broth and sauce. Cover and cook on high
setting one hour; reduce heat to low setting and cook
3-1/2 hours.

2 Add pineapple, green peppers and rice; mix well.
Cover and cook on low setting 1-1/2 more hours.

Serves 4 to 6

CHICKEN & SAUSAGE ÉTOUFFÉE

ROBIN DUSENBERY
SAN ANTONIO, TX

Chicken and sausage replace crawfish in this version of the popular Cajun dish.

1 Heat oil in a Dutch oven over medium heat. Add onion, pepper, celery and chicken; cook until juices run clear when chicken is pierced with a fork.

2 While chicken is cooking, place sausage in a microwave-safe dish with just enough water to cover. Microwave on high 5 minutes; drain sausage and add to chicken mixture.

3 Add tomatoes to chicken mixture; cook 10 minutes over low heat. Add tomato paste and soup; stir until well blended. Simmer 3 minutes or until bubbly. Serve over hot cooked rice.

Serves 4 to 6

1 T. olive oil
1 onion, chopped
1 green pepper, chopped
2 stalks celery, chopped
1 lb. boneless, skinless
   chicken breasts, cubed
1 lb. smoked pork
   sausage, sliced
2 10-oz. cans diced
   tomatoes with green
   chiles
6-oz. can tomato paste
2 10-3/4 oz. cans cream
   of mushroom soup
hot cooked rice

COUNTRY SMOTHERED CHICKEN TENDERS

DEBRA CARABALLO
HUMBLE, TX

I came up with this quick & easy dinner based on a similar dish I had at a favorite restaurant of ours in Bryan, Texas that's no longer in business. We all love this dish.

8 to 10 frozen uncooked breaded chicken tenders

12-oz. pkg. frozen sliced onions and green peppers, divided

2-3/4 oz. pkg. country gravy mix

2 c. water

1 Arrange chicken tenders in a 2-quart casserole dish sprayed with non-stick vegetable spray. Bake, uncovered, at 350 degrees for 20 minutes. Remove from oven. Arrange half of onions and peppers on top; set aside. Reserve remaining vegetables for another recipe. Stir together gravy mix and water, blending well; spoon over casserole. Cover and bake for another 25 to 30 minutes, until chicken and vegetables are tender and gravy has thickened.

Serves 4 to 6

CRISPY POTATO FINGERS

LISA JOHNSON
HALLSVILLE, TX

My mama always made these "tater fingers" for my kids when they would come see her for a visit. The kids are both grown now, and they still love it when Granny makes these yummy potatoes!

3 c. corn flake cereal

3 T. grated Parmesan cheese

1 t. paprika

1/4 t. garlic salt

3 T. butter, melted

2 baking potatoes, peeled and cut into strips

1 Place cereal, cheese and seasonings into a blender or food processor. Process until crushed and well mixed. Pour cereal mixture into a pie plate or shallow dish; place melted butter in a separate shallow dish. Dip potato strips into butter, then into cereal mixture, coating well.

2 Arrange potato strips on a greased baking sheet. Bake at 375 degrees for 25 minutes, or until tender and golden.

Makes 4 servings

COUNTRY HAM & RED-EYE GRAVY

JO ANN
GOOSEBERRY PATCH

This unusual pairing of ingredients is always a pleasant surprise to the ones lucky enough to taste it! Yum!

1 Cut ham slices into serving-size pieces. Make cuts in fat to keep ham from curling.

2 Melt butter in a heavy skillet over low heat; add ham and cook, in batches, 3 to 5 minutes on each side, until lightly browned. Remove ham from skillet and keep warm. Reserve drippings in skillet.

3 Stir brown sugar into hot drippings until dissolved, if desired. Add coffee and bring to a boil; reduce heat and simmer 5 minutes. Serve with ham.

Serves 4 to 6

> 3 1/8 to 1/4-inch-thick slices country ham
> 1/4 c. butter
> Optional: 1/4 c. brown sugar, packed
> 1 c. strong-brewed coffee

IMPOSSIBLY EASY BLT PIE

ATHENA COLEGROVE
BIG SPRINGS, TX

I delighted my family one day with this super-simple meal. We all like BLT's, so we really love this pie!

1 Layer bacon and cheese in a lightly greased 9" pie plate. In a bowl, whisk together baking mix, 1/3 cup mayonnaise, milk, pepper and eggs until blended. Pour over cheese.

2 Bake at 350 degrees for 25 to 30 minutes, until top is golden and a knife inserted in center comes out clean. Let stand 5 minutes. Spread remaining mayonnaise over pie. Sprinkle with lettuce; arrange tomato slices over lettuce.

Serves 6

> 12 slices bacon, crisply cooked and crumbled
> 1 c. shredded Swiss cheese
> 1/2 c. biscuit baking mix
> 1/3 c. plus 2 T. mayonnaise, divided
> 3/4 c. milk
> 1/8 t. pepper
> 2 eggs, beaten
> 1 c. shredded lettuce
> 6 thin slices tomato

DEEP SOUTH CHICKEN & DUMPLINGS

CHRISTIAN BROWN
KILLEEN, TX

This delicious comfort food is our family favorite. I serve it with a fruit salad...perfect!

4-lb. roasting chicken
Supreme Sauce
Dumplings
salt and pepper to taste
Garnish: fresh parsley

1 Bake chicken, covered, in an ungreased roasting pan at 350 degrees for 1-1/2 hours. Let chicken cool while preparing Supreme Sauce. Shred chicken; add to simmering sauce in Dutch oven.

2 Drop Dumplings into sauce by heaping tablespoonfuls. Cover and cook over high heat 10 to 15 minutes, until dumplings are firm and puffy. Discard bay leaves. Add salt and pepper; garnish with fresh parsley.

SUPREME SAUCE:
2 T. butter
1 T. oil
1/2 c. carrot, peeled and diced
1/2 c. celery, diced
3 cloves garlic, minced
2 bay leaves
5 T. all-purpose flour
6 c. chicken broth
1/4 c. milk

1 Melt butter and oil in a Dutch oven over medium heat. Add vegetables, garlic and bay leaves. Sauté until soft.

2 Stir in flour; add broth, one cup at a time, stirring well after each addition. Simmer until thickened; stir in milk.

continued on page 69

1 Mix flour, baking powder and salt. Whisk together eggs and 3/4 cup buttermilk; fold into flour mixture. Stir just until dough forms, adding a little more buttermilk if needed.

Serves 8

DUMPLINGS:
2 c. all-purpose flour
1 T. baking powder
1 t. salt
2 eggs
3/4 to 1 c. buttermilk, divided

EASY BURRITO CASSEROLE

ANGELA LIVELY
CONROE, TX

This dish is so easy and really good...great for dinner on a busy night! Use your favorite frozen burritos and canned chili, along with any extra toppings you like.

1 Spread beans in a greased 13"x9" baking pan. Arrange thawed burritos on top of beans. In a bowl, mix enchilada sauce and chili together. Spoon sauce mixture over burritos; top with cheese. Bake, uncovered, at 375 degrees for 30 minutes, or until bubbly and burritos are cooked through.

Serves 8

2 c. refried black beans
8 frozen burritos, completely thawed
10-1/2 oz. can red enchilada sauce
15-oz. can chili
8-oz. pkg. shredded Monterey Jack cheese

EASY FANCY BROCCOLI

JO ANN
GOOSEBERRY PATCH

What an easy dish to make and it tastes delightful!

2 T. pine nuts
1 T. butter
1 T. olive oil
6 cloves garlic, thinly
 sliced
1 lb. broccoli flowerets
1/8 t. salt
1/8 t. red pepper flakes

1 Toast pine nuts in a large skillet over medium heat 6 minutes, or until golden. Remove from skillet and set aside. Heat butter and oil in same skillet over medium heat until butter melts. Add garlic; sauté one to 2 minutes, or until golden. Add broccoli, salt and red pepper flakes. Sauté 8 minutes, or until broccoli is tender. Stir in pine nuts before serving.

Makes 6 servings

CHICKEN & WILD RICE

KIMBERLY LYONS
COMMERCE, TX

Mmm...great with fresh-baked bread and a green salad.
Freezes beautifully!

2 6.2-oz. pkgs. quick-
 cooking long-grain
 and wild rice mix with
 seasoning packets
4 boneless, skinless
 chicken breasts, cut
 into 1-inch cubes
10-3/4 oz. can cream of
 mushroom soup
1-1/3 c. frozen mixed
 vegetables, thawed
3 c. water

1 Gently stir together all ingredients. Spread into an ungreased 13"x9" baking pan.

2 Bake, uncovered, at 350 degrees for about 45 minutes, stirring occasionally, until juices run clear when chicken is pierced with a fork.

Serves 6 to 8

EASY ROUND STEAK

ASHLEY WHITEHEAD
SIDNEY, TX

Do you like lots of gravy? Use two packages of soup mix and two cans of soup.

1 Place beef in a 4-quart slow cooker. Add soup mix, water and soup. Cover and cook on low setting for 6 to 8 hours.

Serves 5

> 2 to 2-1/2 lbs. beef round steak, cut into serving-size pieces
> 10-3/4 oz. can cream of mushroom soup
> 1/4 c. water
> 1-1/2 oz. pkg. onion soup mix

SWEET POTATO CASSEROLE

DAWN ROMERO
LEWISVILLE, TX

This is great to take to holiday parties or gatherings.

1 In a large bowl, mix together sweet potatoes, 1/3 cup butter and sugar. Stir in eggs and milk. Spoon mixture into a lightly greased 2-quart casserole dish. In a separate bowl, combine remaining butter and other ingredients. Sprinkle mixture over sweet potatoes.

2 Bake, uncovered, at 325 degrees for one hour, or until heated through and bubbly.

Serves 4

> 4 c. mashed sweet potatoes
> 1/3 c. plus 2 T. butter, melted and divided
> 2 T. sugar
> 2 eggs, beaten
> 1/2 c. milk
> 1/3 c. chopped pecans
> 1/3 c. sweetened flaked coconut
> 1/3 c. brown sugar, packed
> 2 T. all-purpose flour

EGG-TOPPED PIZZA

CONNIE HILTY
PEARLAND, TX

Is there anything better than pizza with some meatless protein?
Try this and you'll know what I mean!

11-oz. tube refrigerated thin-crust pizza dough

14-oz. can pizza sauce

16-oz. container ricotta cheese

1/4 c. fresh oregano, snipped

3 T. sun-dried tomatoes, chopped

4 eggs

salt and pepper to taste

1 Roll out dough into a 13-inch by 9-inch rectangle; transfer to a greased rimmed baking sheet. Spread pizza sauce on dough, leaving a 1/2-inch border. Top with cheese, oregano and sun-dried tomatoes. Bake at 500 degrees for 4 to 5 minutes, or until crust begins to turn golden. Crack each egg into a small bowl and slip onto pizza, being careful not to break the yolks. Bake for another 5 minutes, until eggs are done as desired.

Makes 4 servings

BARBECUE CHICKEN KABOBS

ATHENA COLEGROVE
BIG SPRINGS, TX

If you love to barbecue, you'll love these easy-to-make kabobs
that are as pretty as they are tasty!

4 boneless, skinless chicken breasts, cubed

1 green pepper, cut into 2-inch squares

1 sweet onion, cut into wedges

1 red pepper, cut into 2-inch squares

1 c. favorite barbecue sauce

6 skewers

1 Thread chicken, green pepper, onion and red pepper pieces alternately onto skewers. Place kabobs on a lightly oiled grill pan over medium heat.

2 Cook for 12 to 15 minutes, turning and brushing frequently with barbecue sauce, until chicken juices run clear and vegetables are tender.

Serves 6

FIESTA BEEF FAJITAS

SHELLY LIVINGSTON
SHAMROCK, TX

Flavorful skirt steak is traditional in fajitas, but if your grocery doesn't carry it, flank steak is also a good choice.

1 Place beef in a 4-quart slow cooker and set aside.

2 Stir together tomatoes and fajita seasoning mix in a bowl; pour over beef. Cover and cook on high setting one hour; reduce heat to low setting and cook 8 hours.

3 Add onion and green peppers; cover and cook on low setting one more hour. Remove beef and vegetables from slow cooker; shred beef with 2 forks. Serve beef mixture on warmed tortillas with desired garnishes.

Serves 4

2 lbs. beef skirt steak

14-1/2 oz. can diced tomatoes with green chiles

2 1.12-oz. pkgs. fajita seasoning mix

1 onion, vertically sliced

2 green peppers, sliced into strips

8 to 12 10-inch flour tortillas, warmed

Garnishes: guacamole, sour cream, shredded cheese, salsa, shredded lettuce

KITCHEN TIP

Choose whole-grain pizza crusts, pita rounds or flatbreads to make your pizzas a bit more nutritious.

FIESTA CHICKEN

RACHEL HARTER
THE WOODLANDS, TX

*I created this recipe on a whim with ingredients I had
on hand. This dish is a healthy southwestern take on chicken,
and it's so easy to prepare!*

**4 to 6 boneless, skinless
chicken breasts**

**15-1/4 oz. can corn,
drained**

**15-1/2 oz. can black
beans, drained and
rinsed**

16-oz. jar salsa

**Optional: 7-oz. pkg.
Spanish rice mix,
prepared**

**Garnish: shredded
cheese, sliced avocado**

1 Spray a 5-quart slow cooker with non-stick
vegetable spray. Arrange chicken breasts in slow
cooker; top with corn, beans and salsa. Cover
and cook on low setting for 7 to 8 hours, or on
high setting for 4 hours. Stir just before serving. If
desired, serve over Spanish rice; garnish as desired

Makes 4 servings

FRIED GREEN TOMATOES

GINNY SCHNEIDER
MUENSTER, TX

Summer squash or okra can also be prepared using this same batter.

1 c. all-purpose flour

1 c. cornmeal

1/2 t. salt

1/2 t. pepper

3 green tomatoes, sliced

oil for frying

1 Whisk together dry ingredients. Dip tomatoes into
mixture. Pour oil to a depth of 2 inches in a Dutch
oven or cast-iron skillet; heat to 350 degrees. Fry
tomatoes until golden and crispy on both sides.
Drain on paper towels.

Serves 4

CILANTRO CHICKEN IN TORTILLA BOWLS

KRIS AXTELL
JOHNSON CITY, TX

This recipe is a winner for two reasons...I can use my favorite cast-iron skillet, and then serve it in tortilla bowls!

1 Make Tortilla Bowls; set aside. Cook rice according to package directions; keep warm. Meanwhile, in a large skillet over medium-high heat, heat oil. Add chicken, cilantro and garlic. Cook, stirring occasionally, until chicken is no longer pink, about 10 minutes.

2 Remove chicken from skillet; keep warm. Heat remaining oil in same skillet; add onion and pepper. Cook, stirring occasionally, until onion is softened, about 4 minutes. Stir in beans and rice. Continue cooking, stirring occasionally, until heated through. To serve, place lettuce in bottom of prepared Tortilla Bowl. Spoon rice mixture on top and add chicken. Serve with hot sauce.

3 For each Tortilla Bowl, use one tortilla. Spray each side of the tortilla with cooking oil spray. Set desired number of oven-proof soup bowls upside-down on a baking sheet. Drape tortilla over the outside of each bowl. Bake at 350 degrees for just a few minutes, until lightly golden. Let stand until cooled before removing from soup bowls.

Makes 4 servings

1 c. long-cooking rice, uncooked

3 T. canola oil, divided

1 lb. boneless, skinless chicken breasts, cubed

1 T. fresh cilantro, chopped

1 T. garlic, finely minced

1 c. onion, chopped

1/2 red pepper, chopped

15-oz. can red beans, drained and rinsed

3 c. shredded lettuce

Optional: additional chopped cilantro

hot pepper sauce

4 10-inch flour tortillas

GOLDEN MACARONI & CHEESE

GALE HARRIS
FORT WORTH, TX

A topping of crispy French fried onions gives this traditional standby extra crunch.

10-3/4 oz. can cream of
  mushroom soup
1/2 c. milk
1/2 t. mustard
1/8 t. pepper
3 c. elbow macaroni,
  cooked
2 c. shredded Cheddar
  cheese, divided
1 c. French fried onions

1 Blend soup, milk, mustard and pepper in a lightly greased 1-1/2 quart casserole dish. Stir in macaroni and 1-1/2 cups cheese. Bake, uncovered, at 350 degrees for 20 minutes. Top with remaining cheese and onions; bake 10 additional minutes.

Serves 4

GREAT NANA'S BEER ROAST

CHERYL MASON
SUGAR LAND, TX

I love keeping family recipes alive! This recipe comes from my husband's grandma. It's our son's favorite. It is also good made in a slow cooker. Serve the sauce over noodles...delicious!

3 to 4-lb. boneless beef
  chuck roast
salt and pepper to taste
1 onion, sliced
12-oz. can beer (not light
  beer)
1/3 c. chili sauce
3 T. brown sugar,
  packed
1 clove garlic, minced

1 Season roast with salt and pepper; place in a large roasting pan. Cover with onion slices. Combine remaining ingredients in a bowl; spoon over roast. Cover and bake at 350 degrees for 3-1/2 hours, basting occasionally with pan juices, until roast is tender. May also be prepared in a 6-quart slow cooker. Cover and cook on low setting for 6 to 8 hours, basting occasionally with cooking juices.

Serves 6

DADDY'S SHEPHERD'S PIE

SHEILA WAKEMAN
WINNSBORO, TX

My dad grew up eating this dish. I can remember going to Dad's house on the weekends (he was a single dad) and we would make this together. Now my daughter and I make it together too.

1 Brown beef in a skillet over medium heat; drain. Stir in soup and water; simmer until heated through. Meanwhile, prepare potato flakes as package directs; set aside.

2 Place beef mixture in a 13"x9" baking pan sprayed with non-stick vegetable spray. Top with corn; spread potatoes evenly across top. Sprinkle with cheese.

3 Bake, uncovered, at 425 degrees for about 10 minutes, until hot and cheese is melted.

Makes 6 to 8 servings

1 lb. ground beef

10-3/4 oz. can cream of mushroom soup

2/3 c. water

7.2-oz. pkg. homestyle creamy butter-flavored instant mashed potato flakes

2 c. corn

8-oz. pkg. shredded Cheddar cheese

GREEK PITA PIZZAS

**LYNDA MCCORMICK
BURKBURNETT, TX**

*These are my healthy go-to summer pizzas. Kids and adults love
them! For a crisper crust, spritz pitas with olive oil spray and a
pinch of coarse salt, then broil for one to 2 minutes before adding
the toppings.*

10-oz. pkg. frozen
  chopped spinach,
  thawed and well
  drained
4 green onions, chopped
chopped fresh dill to
  taste
4 whole-wheat pita
  rounds, split
4 roma tomatoes, sliced
  1/2-inch thick
1/2 c. crumbled feta
  cheese with basil &
  tomato
dried oregano or Greek
  seasoning to taste

1 Mix spinach, onions and dill in a small bowl.
Season with garlic salt and pepper; set aside.
Place pita rounds on ungreased baking sheets.
Arrange tomato slices among pitas. Spread spinach
mixture evenly over tomatoes; spread cheese over
tomatoes. Sprinkle with desired seasoning. Bake at
450 degrees for 10 to 15 minutes, until crisp. Cut
into wedges.

Makes 8 servings

TEXAS TRIVIA

In parts of Texas, Christmas tamales
are a classic holiday treat, as
families get together to carry on the
tamale-making traditions.

SUPER-EASY STUFFED PEPPERS

TABETHA MOORE
NEW BRAUNFELS, TX

My husband says these are the best peppers!

1 Bring a large saucepan of water to a boil; add peppers and boil until tender. Drain and set aside. Brown ground beef with onion in a skillet; drain. Add Italian seasoning and garlic. Set aside 1/2 cup spaghetti sauce.

2 Combine ground beef mixture, remaining sauce, cooked rice, salt and pepper in a bowl. Arrange peppers in a lightly greased 8"x8" baking pan. Fill peppers completely with ground beef mixture, spooning any extra mixture between peppers. Top with reserved sauce. Add pepper tops if using. Lightly cover with aluminum foil; bake at 400 degrees for 20 to 25 minutes. Sprinkle with Parmesan cheese.

Serves 4

- 4 green, red or orange peppers, tops removed
- 1 lb. ground beef
- 1 onion, diced
- 1 T. Italian seasoning
- 1 clove garlic, pressed
- 26-oz. can spaghetti sauce, divided
- 3 c. cooked brown rice
- salt and pepper to taste
- Garnish: shredded Parmesan cheese

GREEN CHILE RICE

DEBBIE WILSON
WEATHERFORD, TX

Sprinkle with diced jalapeño peppers for an extra kick!

1 Combine all ingredients in an ungreased 2-quart casserole dish. Mix well. Bake, uncovered, at 400 degrees until bubbly, about 20 minutes.

Serves 6

- 4 c. cooked rice
- 8-oz. pkg. shredded mozzarella cheese
- 2 c. sour cream
- 4-oz. can diced green chiles, drained

RED DUMPLINGS

ELIZABETH ONG
PORTER, TX

My family loves this biscuit-topped skillet dinner! I can remember eating it when I was very little and my grandmother fixed it for us. Mama wrote on the recipe card that it was from 1950.

1 lb. ground beef
1/2 lb. ground pork sausage
2 green peppers, sliced into rings
1 onion, sliced and separated into rings
46-oz. can cocktail vegetable juice
1 to 2 12-oz. cans refrigerated biscuits, depending on skillet size
salt and pepper to taste

1 Mix beef and sausage in a bowl; form into 4 patties. Brown patties in a skillet over medium heat. Drain; add green peppers and onion to skillet on top of patties. Pour in vegetable juice to completely cover patties. Bring to a boil; cover and reduce heat to a simmer for 30 minutes.

2 Arrange enough biscuits to cover mixture in skillet; spoon juice over biscuits. Cover and cook an additional 10 minutes, or until biscuits are done. Add salt and pepper as desired.

Serves 4

Apple-Walnut Chicken Salad, p. 24

Whether you are looking for a quick-to-make breakfast dish, no-fuss party fare, satisfying soups and sandwiches, main dishes to fill them up, or a sweet little something to savor at the end of the meal, you'll love these recipes from the amazing cooks in the great state of **Texas**.

Brats, Taters & Apples, p. 58

Buttermilk Cinnamon Rolls, p. 11

Cheesy Chicken & Noodle Soup, p. 27

Chicken & Wild Rice, p. 70

Benson's Ultimate Pancakes, p. 9

Chocolate Chip-Oat Cookies, p.128

Chocolate Oat Cupcakes, p.131

Double Peanut Cookies, p.134

Easy Round Steak, p. 71

Zippy Shredded Pork, p. 54

Egg & Bacon Quesadillas, p.13

Emma's Gingerbread Muffins, p.14

Erma Lee's Chicken Soup, p. 29

Fresh Fruit Salsa, p. 115

Fruit Compote, p. 32

Glazed Cocktail Sausages, p. 114

Greek Pita Pizzas, p. 78

Green Chile Rice, p. 79

Hot Chocolate Supreme, p. 110

Huevos Rancheros to Go-Go, p. 15

Impossibly Easy BLT Pie, p. 67

Lynda's Spinach-Feta Dip, p. 119

Lynda's Salmon Burgers, p. 38

Lisa's Chicken Tortilla Soup, p. 39

Mini Spinach & Bacon Quiches, p. 120

Muffuletta Sandwich, p. 40

Pecan Bites, p. 122

Roasted Veggie Panini, p. 43

Soft Pumpkin Cookies, p. 145

Sweet Potato Casserole, p. 71

Texas Toads in the Hole, p. 18

Texas 2-Step, p. 31

The Ultimate Shrimp Sandwich, p. 30

Toss-It-Together Salsa, p. 108

SHRIMP & BEAN BURRITO BOWLS

MARIA GOMEZ
EL PASO, TX

We often serve this with warm tortillas and extra chili sauce.

1 In a large saucepan over medium heat, bring broth and beans to a simmer. Cook for 10 minutes, stirring occasionally.

2 Transfer bean mixture to a bowl; add butter, 1/4 teaspoon salt and 1/4 teaspoon pepper. Mash until smooth; set aside. Sprinkle shrimp with remaining salt and pepper.

3 Add oil to a skillet over medium heat. Add shrimp and cook for 4 minutes, turning after 2 minutes. Remove from heat; stir in chili sauce. To serve, divide bean mixture and rice among 4 bowls. Top with shrimp, cilantro and avocado; sprinkle with cheese. Serve with lime wedges.

Makes 4 servings

3/4 c. chicken broth

2 15-1/2 oz. cans kidney beans, drained and rinsed

1-1/2 T. butter

1/2 t. salt, divided

1/2 t. pepper, divided

1 lb. medium shrimp, peeled and cleaned

2 t. olive oil

1-1/2 T. sweet chili sauce

2 c. cooked brown rice, warmed

1 T. fresh cilantro, chopped

1 avocado, peeled, pitted and sliced

2 T. crumbled cotija cheese or shredded Parmesan cheese

Garnish: 4 lime wedges

MEMA JEANETTE'S BAKED CORN

CINDY KEMP
LAKE JACKSON, TX

Absolutely decadent! I first tasted this bit of heaven in 2002 at my husband's step-mother's home. Mema Jeanette completely stole my heart with her gentle, kind ways and, of course, her amazing cooking skills. Mema has gone on to be with the Lord, but every time I make this side dish, every member of the family smiles at her wonderful memory. Fresh corn is really the best for this!

8 to 10 ears sweet corn

1/2 c. butter, sliced

16-oz. pkg. frozen creamed corn, thawed, or 14-3/4 oz. can creamed corn

1/4 c. sugar

2 T. all-purpose flour

salt and pepper to taste

1 c. half-and-half or milk

Optional: additional 1/2 c. butter, melted

1 Cut kernels from cobs and blanch in boiling water. Drain; transfer to a large bowl and set aside.

2 Place butter in a 2-quart casserole dish; set in the oven at 350 degrees, until melted. Meanwhile, add creamed corn, sugar, flour, seasonings and half-and-half or milk to corn. Mix well, being careful not to mash the corn.

3 Carefully remove casserole dish from oven; pour corn mixture into dish. If desired, drizzle with additional butter. Bake, uncovered, at 350 degrees for 45 to 50 minutes, until bubbly and edges are golden. Remove from oven and let stand for about 20 minutes, until thickened slightly.

Makes 6 to 8 servings

MOM'S SPAGHETTI & MEATBALLS

ELAINE LUCAS
RUNGE, TX

Sometimes I like to serve this with whole-grain spaghetti and sometimes with spiralized zucchini...both are delicious!

1 In a large skillet over medium-low heat, combine tomato sauce and seasonings. Bring to a simmer. Meanwhile, make Meatballs. Add uncooked meatballs to sauce. Simmer over medium-low heat for about 30 minutes, turning occasionally, until meatballs are no longer pink in the center.

2 Serve sauce and meatballs over spaghetti or zucchini. Garnish with Parmesan cheese.

2 8-oz. cans tomato sauce
1/2 t. garlic powder
1/2 t. dried oregano
1/2 t. dried basil
salt and pepper to taste
Meatballs
16-oz. pkg. whole-wheat spaghetti, cooked, or blanched spiralized or shaved zucchini
Garnish: shredded Parmesan cheese

1 Combine all ingredients in a large bowl; mix well. Form into 2-inch balls.

Serves 6

MEATBALLS:
1 lb. lean ground beef
3 T. shredded Parmesan cheese
2 eggs, beaten
1 slice white bread, crumbled
1/2 t. garlic salt

KICKIN' PORK CHOPS

AMY WOODS
COLLINSVILLE, TX

I love these quick & easy chops! My son Stephen puts them on when he gets home from high school. I simply add sides like boiled new potatoes and steamed Brussels sprouts for a healthy weeknight meal we enjoy.

4 to 6 thick-cut boneless pork chops
10-3/4 oz. can cream of chicken soup
1-oz. pkg. ranch salad dressing mix
1 T. Creole seasoning

1 Spray a slow cooker with non-stick vegetable spray. Lay pork chops in slow cooker and set aside. Mix remaining ingredients in a bowl; spoon over pork chops. Cover and cook on low setting for 4 to 5 hours, until pork chops are tender.

Makes 4 to 6 servings

ROASTED OKRA FRIES

SONIA HAWKINS
AMARILLO, TX

I love okra cooked this way and it is healthier than fried okra! We use this recipe to roast cauliflower, broccoli, zucchini, yellow squash and Brussels sprouts. Asparagus too...sprinkle with 1/4 cup grated Parmesan cheese the last 5 minutes of roasting. Yum! .

1 lb. fresh okra
2 T. olive oil
1/4 t. garlic powder
salt and pepper to taste

1 Rinse okra and pat dry with a paper towel. Trim off stem ends; cut okra into slices and place in a large bowl. Drizzle with olive oil and toss to coat well. Sprinkle with seasonings. Spread okra on an oiled 17"x12" jelly-roll pan. Bake at 425 degrees for 20 minutes, or until okra is crisp and golden.

Serves 4

LEEA'S QUICK SPAGHETTI

LEEA MERCER
LEAGUE CITY, TX

My kids love this...it's delicious and very budget-friendly too!

1 Cook spaghetti according to package directions; drain. Meanwhile, brown beef and onion in a skillet over medium heat; drain. Add salt and pepper; stir in tomato sauce, tomato paste, garlic and seasonings. If too thick, add a little water. Reduce heat to low. Simmer for 20 to 30 minutes, stirring occasionally. Serve sauce over spaghetti.

Serves 4

7-oz. pkg. spaghetti, uncooked
1 lb. ground beef
1/2 c. onion, diced
salt and pepper to taste
2 8-oz. cans tomato sauce
6-oz. can tomato paste
3 cloves garlic, minced
2 to 3 T. dried basil
1 to 2 t. dried oregano

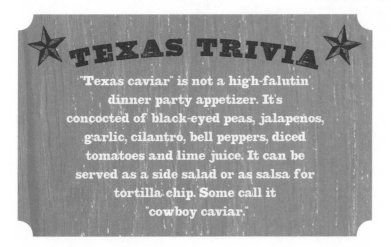

TEXAS TRIVIA

"Texas caviar" is not a high-falutin' dinner party appetizer. It's concocted of black-eyed peas, jalapeños, garlic, cilantro, bell peppers, diced tomatoes and lime juice. It can be served as a side salad or as salsa for tortilla chip. Some call it "cowboy caviar."

MOM'S TAMALE PIE

**JOAN CHANCE
HOUSTON, TX**

*My mom was ahead of her time. Instead of fixing the usual meat
& potato dishes, we learned to eat Tex-Mex before it was popular!
Before polenta, too...we knew it as cornmeal mush.*

**5 c. water, divided
1 t. salt
1 c. cornmeal
2 T. butter
1/4 c. onion, chopped
1/2 c. green pepper,
   chopped
1 clove garlic, minced
1 lb. ground beef
1 T. all-purpose flour
2 t. chili powder, or more
   to taste
1/8 t. pepper
2-1/2 c. tomatoes,
   chopped
1/2 c. sliced black olives,
   drained**

1 In a large saucepan over medium heat, bring
4 cups water to a boil; add salt. In a bowl, mix
cornmeal with remaining cold water; slowly add
to boiling water. Cook and stir over low heat until
thickened, about 15 minutes. Remove from heat;
set aside.

2 Melt butter in a large skillet over medium heat;
add onion, green pepper and garlic. Cook for
3 minutes. Set mixture aside in a bowl; brown beef
in the same skillet, until no longer pink. Return onion
mixture to skillet along with remaining ingredients;
stir well. Spoon a thin layer of cooked cornmeal into
a lightly greased 2-quart casserole dish. Top with
beef mixture; spread remaining cornmeal on top in
a thin layer.

3 Bake, uncovered, at 350 degrees for one hour,
or until heated through and golden on top.

Makes 6 to 8 servings

MUSTARD-GLAZED PORK TENDERLOIN

JO ANN
GOOSEBERRY PATCH

The combination of the mustard and the orange juice is just perfect or these pork chops...and the Cajun seasoning adds just the right kick. These take few ingredients but are so delicious!

1 Stir together first 3 ingredients. Place pork in a shallow dish or a plastic zipping bag; pour mustard mixture over pork. Cover or seal and chill at least 30 minutes, turning occasionally.

2 Preheat grill to medium-high heat. Remove pork from marinade, discarding marinade.

3 Grill, covered with grill lid, 10 to 12 minutes on each side or until a meat thermometer inserted into thickest portion registers 155 degrees. Remove from grill; let stand until thermometer registers 160 degrees. Let stand 5 more minutes before slicing into chops.

4 to 6 servings

1 c. Dijon mustard
1/3 c. orange juice
2 T. Cajun seasoning
1-1/2 lbs. pork tenderloin

NANA'S SLOW-COOKER MEATBALLS

STEPHANIE NORTON
SAGINAW, TX

These meatballs are wonderful with your favorite pasta but they are also delightful all by themselves with a green salad and some Texas toast. Enjoy!

2-1/2 c. catsup
1 c. brown sugar, packed
2 T. Worcestershire sauce
2 lbs. ground beef
1.35-oz. pkg. onion soup mix
5-oz. can evaporated milk

1 Combine catsup, brown sugar and Worcestershire sauce in a 4-quart slow cooker; stir well and cover. Turn slow cooker to high setting and allow mixture to warm while preparing the meatballs.

2 Combine beef, onion soup mix and evaporated milk; mix well and form into one-inch balls. Place meatballs on an ungreased 15"x10" jelly-roll pan. Bake at 325 degrees for 20 minutes; drain. Spoon meatballs into slow cooker and reduce setting to low. Cover and cook 2 to 3 hours, stirring gently after one hour.

Makes 4 dozen

POOR MAN'S CORDON BLEU

LINDA LAMB
ROUND ROCK, TX

A quick & easy variation on a classic.

1 For each turkey roll, lay out 2 turkey slices, overlapping ends by 2 to 3 inches. Add a ham slice, centered on turkey slices. Place 2 cheese slices on top, with ends barely touching. Roll up, starting on one short side. Repeat with remaining ingredients to make 8 rolls. Dip rolls into water to moisten. Coat in bread crumbs, reserving 1/4 cup bread crumbs for topping. Place rolls seam-side down in a greased 13"x9" baking pan. Sprinkle reserved crumbs on top. Bake, uncovered, at 350 degrees for 15 to 20 minutes, until lightly golden and cheese is melted.

Serves 4

16 slices deli turkey
8 slices deli ham
16 slices Swiss cheese
1/2 c. water
2 c. Italian-flavored dry bread crumbs, divided

POPPY SEED CHICKEN

CINDY BUNCH
POTTSBORO, TX

This is a great make-and-freeze dish. I usually double the recipe and keep one in the freezer. If you want to do this, leave the crackers, butter and poppy seed off until ready to bake.

1 In a large bowl, combine chicken, soup and sour cream; mix well. Spread in a 13"x9" baking pan sprayed with non-stick vegetable spray. Spread crushed crackers over top; drizzle with melted butter and sprinkle with poppy seed.

2 Cover with aluminum foil. Bake at 350 degrees for 30 to 45 minutes, until bubbly at the edges. Remove foil; bake an additional 10 to 15 minutes, until crackers are toasted and golden.

Makes 4 to 6 servings

6 boneless, skinless chicken breasts, cooked and cut into bite-size pieces
23-oz. can cream of chicken soup
16-oz. container sour cream
1 sleeve round buttery crackers, crushed
1/2 c. butter
Garnish: poppy seed to taste

 ALL-TIME-FAVORITE RECIPES FROM TEXAS COOKS **95**

PEPPER CHICKEN

TRACEY REGNOLD
LEWISVILLE, TX

*This was my mother's recipe and I have modified it to fit our family.
It's a favorite at our house. This dish can be made with beef too.*

1 onion, chopped

1 green pepper, chopped

1 to 2 cloves garlic, chopped

2 to 3 T. olive oil

4 boneless, skinless chicken breasts, cubed

3/4 c. white wine or chicken broth

10-3/4 oz. can cream of mushroom soup

10-3/4 oz. can golden mushroom soup

1/2 c. chicken broth

salt and pepper to taste

cooked rice or egg noodles

1 In a skillet over medium heat, sauté onion, green pepper and garlic in oil until onion is translucent, 2 to 3 minutes. Add chicken and cook until golden about 3 to 4 minutes; drain. Add wine or broth and cook for one to 2 minutes. Add soups, broth, salt and pepper, stirring well to combine.

2 Simmer over medium-low heat for about 10 minutes. Serve over hot cooked rice or noodles.

Serves 4 to 8

TEXAS HASH

MATTIE AXTELL
AMARILLO, TX

You'll love this hearty chili-like dish! I like to serve it with a fresh green salad and a big glass of sweet tea.

1 Brown beef with onion and red or green pepper in a skillet over medium heat; drain. Stir in uncooked rice and remaining ingredients except garnish.

2 Cover and simmer over low heat 25 minutes, or until water is absorbed and rice is tender. Garnish with fresh thyme sprigs.

Makes 6 servings

1-1/2 lb. ground beef
1 small onion, diced
1 red pepper, diced
1 c. long-cooking brown rice, uncooked
14-1/2 oz. can diced tomatoes
2 c. water
2 t. chili powder
1 t. paprika
1/4 t. salt
1/4 t. pepper
Garnish: fresh thyme sprigs

TEXAS TRIVIA

Nearly all Texas foods over time have been influenced by Spanish, Mexican and Native American techniques. Plus, there are Creole and Cajun details worked into the landscape, along with German, Czech and Jewish overtones.

QUICK- AS- A-WINK CHICKEN & DUMPLIN'S

TRACIE CARLSON
RICHARDSON, TX

An excellent quick remedy for cold sufferers...just add lots of freshly minced garlic!

8 c. chicken broth or water

2 T. chicken bouillon granules

4 to 6 cloves garlic, minced

1 lb. boneless, skinless chicken breast tenders

16-oz. tube refrigerated flaky biscuits

Garnish: dried parsley

1 Bring broth or water to a boil in a stockpot over high heat; add bouillon and garlic. Reduce heat to medium; add chicken tenders. Simmer for 10 minutes.

2 Separate biscuits and tear each biscuit into 3 or 4 pieces. Drop biscuit pieces into simmering broth mixture; reduce heat to low. Continue cooking at a low simmer for another 15 to 20 minutes, until chicken and biscuit pieces are cooked through. Sprinkle with parsley before serving.

Makes 6 servings

KITCHEN TIP

An easy way to crumble ground beef is to use a potato masher. It makes browning so quick & easy.

RANCH-STYLE BEEF & BEAN DINNER

LEEA MERCER
EDNA, TX

This is a quick & easy recipe! Very yummy served with cornbread.

1 Brown beef and onion in a skillet over medium heat. Drain; season with salt and pepper. Stir in beans and garlic; heat through.

Makes 4 servings

1 lb. ground beef
1/2 c. onion, chopped
salt and pepper to taste
2 15-oz. cans ranch-style beans
2 to 3 cloves garlic, minced

SPANISH RICE

LYNDA MCCORMICK
BURKBURNETT, TX

I love this easy stovetop version of an old favorite…you will too!

1 Heat oil in a 12" skillet; add rice, heating until golden. Add garlic; sauté for one minute. Mix in undrained tomatoes, broth, onion and green pepper; bring to a boil. Reduce heat; cover and simmer until rice is done, about 15 minutes. Remove from heat; stir in cilantro.

Serves 6

3 T. olive oil
1 c. long-cooking rice, uncooked
2 to 3 cloves garlic, minced
16-oz. can Mexican-style tomatoes, chopped
1/2 c. chicken broth
1/2 c. red onion, chopped
1/4 c. green pepper, chopped
1/2 c. fresh cilantro, chopped

LEMON WINE CHICKEN SKILLET

JUDY YOUNG
PLANO, TX

This is one of my family's all-time favorite chicken recipes. It is so easy to make and tastes phenomenal! Serve with steamed brown rice or your favorite pasta.

4 boneless, skinless chicken breasts

lemon pepper to taste

1 egg

1/2 c. lemon-flavored white cooking wine, divided

1/4 c. all-purpose flour

6 T. butter, divided

2 to 3 T. capers

Garnish: chopped fresh parsley

1 Flatten chicken breasts slightly between 2 pieces of wax paper. Season chicken with lemon pepper. In a small bowl, lightly beat egg with 2 tablespoons wine. Place flour in a separate shallow bowl. Dip chicken in egg mixture, then in flour to coat.

2 Melt 3 tablespoons butter in a large skillet over medium heat; add chicken. Cook until golden on both sides and no longer pink in the center, about 6 minutes on each side. Transfer chicken to a serving dish. Add remaining wine and butter to drippings in skillet; cook and stir until butter melts. Add capers; heat through. To serve, spoon sauce from the skillet over chicken; sprinkle with parsley.

Serves 4

SUNDAY CHICKEN CASSEROLE

ARLENE COURY
SAN ANTONIO, TX

*My grandmother would prepare this special dish for holidays and
when company was coming. It is the best chicken casserole
I have ever tasted...we always made sure we got a helping before
it disappeared!*

1 In a large stockpot over medium heat, cover
chicken with water. Cook until chicken juices run
clear, 20 to 25 minutes. Drain chicken, reserving
1-3/4 cups broth. Let chicken cool. Cut into bite-
size pieces, discarding skin and bones; set aside.
Toss stuffing mix with melted butter until moistened.
Spread half of stuffing mixture in a lightly greased
11"x8" baking pan; place chicken on top. Blend
reserved broth, soup and sour cream until smooth;
fold in pickle and onion. Pour over chicken; cover
with remaining stuffing mix. Bake, uncovered, at
350 degrees for 20 to 30 minutes, until bubbly. Let
stand 10 minutes before serving.

Serves 6

3 to 4 chicken breasts

6-oz. pkg. herb-flavored
stuffing mix

1/2 c. butter, melted

10-3/4 oz. can cream of
chicken soup

16-oz. container sour
cream

1/4 c. dill pickle, chopped

1 white onion, chopped

CHEESY SAUSAGE-POTATO CASSEROLE

J.J. PRESLEY
PORTLAND, TX

Add some fresh green beans too, if you like.

1 Layer potatoes, sausage and onion in an
oven-proof skillet sprayed with non-stick vegetable
spray. Dot with butter; sprinkle with cheese. Bake at
350 degrees for 1-1/2 hours.

Serves 6 to 8

3 to 4 potatoes, sliced

2 8-oz. links sausage,
sliced into 2-inch
lengths

1 onion, chopped

1/2 c. butter, sliced

1 c. shredded Cheddar
cheese

SOUTHWEST SCALLOPED POTATOES

JOANN KURTZ
WICHITA FALLS, TX

I love it when Hatch green chile season comes around! Our local market has a fellow out in front of the market who will roast them by the pound for you, but you can substitute canned green chiles if needed. These are great with barbecued pork loin or ribs...or any barbecue, really!

2 baking potatoes, sliced
3/4 c. onion, chopped
2 Hatch green chiles, roasted, peeled and seeded, or 4-oz. can chopped green chiles
10-oz. can enchilada sauce
1 c. shredded Monterey Jack cheese

1 Spray a 13"x9" baking pan with non-stick vegetable spray. In pan, layer half of each ingredient, ending with cheese. Repeat layers; cover with aluminum foil. Bake at 350 degrees for 40 minutes; remove foil. Bake another 10 to 15 minutes, until cheese is melted and golden.

Makes 8 to 10 servings

FOOD FOR THOUGHT

Part of the secret of success in life is to eat what you like and let the food fight it out inside. —Mark Twain

SARAH'S TUNA CASSEROLE SUPREME

TRACEY REGNOLD
LEWISVILLE, TX

This good old-fashioned dish started with my mother's recipe. My daughter, Sarah, and I made it our own with a few tweaks. The ingredients are usually in our pantry, so it's easy to make anytime.

1 Cook noodles as package directs; drain and set aside. Meanwhile, in a large skillet over medium heat, sauté onion and celery in butter until translucent. Add cooked noodles to skillet; stir in tuna, soups and cheese spread. Cook until blended and cheese is melted, one to 2 minutes. Stir in peas.

2 Transfer to a lightly greased 13"x9" baking pan; top with Cheddar cheese. Bake, uncovered, at 350 degrees for 20 to 25 minutes, until hot and bubbly. Top with crushed potato chips. Return to oven and bake an additional 5 to 10 minutes, until chips are golden.

Makes 4 to 6 servings

16-oz. pkg. wide egg noodles, uncooked
1 onion, chopped
1/2 c. celery, chopped
1 to 2 T. butter
2 6-oz. cans tuna, drained
10-3/4 oz. can cream of mushroom soup
10-3/4 oz. can golden mushroom soup
1/2 lb. pasteurized process cheese spread, cubed
15-1/4 oz. can peas, drained
1 c. shredded Cheddar cheese
1 c. potato chips, crushed
salt and pepper to taste

JANET SUE'S CRAB CAKES

JANET SUE BURNS
GRANBURY, TX

Lump crabmeat, whole pieces of white crabmeat, is the preferred choice for crab cakes. Serve these cakes with a squeeze of lemon or your favorite sauce to enhance the cakes' delicate flavor.

3 lbs. fresh crabmeat
1-1/4 c. mayonnaise
3 eggs, beaten
1/4 c. onion, minced
3/4 t. seasoned salt
1/8 t. pepper
2 T. dry mustard
3/4 c. pimentos, diced
1 c. green pepper, diced
1 T. Worcestershire sauce
1-1/4 c. dry bread crumbs
Optional: lemon wedges

1 Separate and flake the crabmeat with a fork; set aside.

2 Combine mayonnaise and next 8 ingredients in a bowl. Add crabmeat; mix well. Fold in bread crumbs; divide into 16 portions and shape into patties.

3 Arrange on an ungreased baking sheet and bake at 425 degrees for 10 to 15 minutes, or until golden. Serve with lemon wedges, if desired.

Makes 16

HEARTY LIMA BEAN CASSEROLE

**MARILYN GABLER
FORT WORTH, TX**

*I like to use fresh herbs from my herb garden in this original recipe.
Chock-full of sour cream and cheese, it's a great cool-weather dish.*

1 Place dried beans in a 4-quart slow cooker; add broth and water. Cover and cook on high setting for about 4 hours. Reduce heat to low; continue cooking for 2 hours, or until beans are tender but not mushy. If too dry, add a little more broth. Drain beans; transfer to a greased 3-quart casserole dish. Add onion, sour cream and seasonings; top with cheese. Bake, uncovered, at 375 degrees for 30 minutes, or until hot and bubbly.

Serves 4

2 c. dried lima beans
2 c. vegetable broth
1 c. water
1/2 yellow onion, diced
8-oz. container sour cream
garlic powder to taste
chopped fresh oregano to taste
Garnish: 1/2 c. shredded Cheddar cheese

HONEY-KISSED ACORN SQUASH

**LYNDA MCCORMICK
BURKBURNETT, TX**

*Select acorn squash that's firm, unblemished and feels heavy for its size.
A cut squash will keep in the fridge up to one week. Uncut, it will stay
fresh for one month in a cool, dark place.*

1 Place squash halves, cut-side up, in a microwave-safe dish; microwave on high 8 to 10 minutes, or until tender. Combine pineapple and next 4 ingredients; spoon into squash halves. Microwave on high 30 to 45 seconds, or until thoroughly heated and lightly glazed. Sprinkle with nutmeg, if desired.

Serves 4

2 acorn squash, halved lengthwise and seeded
8-oz. can crushed pineapple, drained
1/4 c. chopped pecans
1/4 c. sweetened dried cranberries
1/4 c. plus 2 T. honey
1/4 c. butter, melted
Optional: nutmeg

CHAPTER FOUR

BIG STYLE

Party Time

YOUR RECIPES WILL BE THE
LIFE OF THE PARTY WHEN YOU
CREATE THESE EASY-TO-MAKE
AND YUMMY-TO-EAT,
TEXAS-STYLE DISHES.

AMARETTO CHEESE SPREAD

JUDY HENFEY
CIBOLO, TX

*A simple recipe for the Christmas or New Year's appetizer table. Serve
with thinly sliced apples and pears. Delicious!*

8-oz. pkg. cream cheese,
softened
1/4 c. amaretto liqueur,
or 1/2 to 1 t. almond
extract
2-1/2 oz. pkg. slivered
almonds
1-1/2 t. butter

1 In a bowl, blend together cream cheese and
liqueur or extract. Form into a ball; wrap in plastic
wrap. Chill until firm. In a small skillet, sauté
almonds in butter over medium heat. Shortly before
serving time, roll ball in almonds. Serve at room
temperature.

Makes 4 to 6 servings

TOSS-IT-TOGETHER SALSA

NICHOLE SULLIVAN
SANTA FE, TX

*Grab a few pantry staples and whip up this last-minute appetizer…
don't forget the tortilla chips!*

2 14-1/2 oz. cans petite-
diced tomatoes
1 onion, diced
1 t. garlic, chopped
1/3 c. pickled jalapeños,
minced
salt and pepper to taste

1 Combine tomatoes with juice and remaining
ingredients in a small bowl; stir well. Serve
immediately or, if preferred, cover and chill
overnight.

Serves 16

AUNT MAXINE'S CHEESE LOGS

LISA BARBER
TYLER, TX

My Aunt Maxine used to make this cheesy treat every year during the holiday. We all looked forward to it. She was a great cook and loved to cook during the holidays. Now my mom makes the cheese logs too...every time I take a bite, I think about my aunt.

1 Place cheeses in the top of a double boiler. Heat over boiling water until melted; stir well. Add pecans and garlic powder; stir well until smooth.

2 Sprinkle chili powder generously on a piece of wax paper; set aside. With your hands, shape cheese mixture into 2 logs, each 8 to 10 inches long. Roll both logs in chili powder, coating well. Wrap logs in wax paper or plastic wrap. Refrigerate overnight, or until firm. Slice and serve.

Serves 8 to 10

8-oz. pkg. cream
  cheese, softened
16-oz. pkg. Colby
  cheese, shredded
1 c. chopped pecans
1 t. garlic powder
chili powder to taste

CHICKEN & RANCH DIP

STACY LUHRS
SOUTHLAKE, TX

This is the perfect spicy, healthy dip! It's always requested whenever I am going to a house dinner party. It is a must at our huge high school tailgates as well. My friends simply refer to it as "The Dip."

2 12-1/2 oz. cans chicken breast, drained
8-oz. container plain Greek yogurt
3 T. ranch salad dressing mix
1/2 c. buffalo wing sauce
1/2 c. shredded Cheddar cheese

1 In a bowl, combine all ingredients except cheese; mix well. Transfer to a lightly greased one-quart casserole dish; top with cheese. Bake, uncovered, at 350 degrees for 20 minutes, until heated through and cheese is melted.

Serves 10

HOT CHOCOLATE SUPREME

LISA ALLBRIGHT
CROCKETT, TX

Curl up and enjoy a mug of this chocolatey cocoa on a frosty winter's day.

1 c. sugar
1/2 c. baking cocoa
1/4 t. salt
5 c. water
2 c. milk
1 c. whipping cream
Garnishes: mini marshmallows or whipped topping, peppermint sticks

1 Combine sugar, cocoa and salt in a saucepan; whisk in water. Bring to a boil over high heat, stirring until sugar is completely dissolved. Reduce heat to medium; add milk and cream. Heat through and keep warm over low heat. If desired, serve topped with marshmallows or whipped topping and peppermint sticks.

Serves 6

CRISPY CHEESE CRACKERS

JENNY MARTIN
PLANO, TX

This is one of our favorite cheese crackers. It is an easier version of a Cheese Straws recipe from my grandmother. I remember my mom making them for her bridge group. Now I make them for my bunko group! The recipe makes a lot, freezes well and tastes delicious.

1 Place cereal or nuts in a bowl; set aside. In a separate bowl, combine remaining ingredients. Mix well and roll into marble-size balls; roll in cereal or nuts to coat.

2 Place balls on a lightly greased baking sheet; flatten gently with a fork. Bake at 350 degrees for 15 to 20 minutes, until crisp and golden.

Makes about 5 dozen

2 c. crispy rice cereal, or 1 c. finely chopped nuts
8-oz. pkg. shredded Cheddar cheese
1 c. butter, softened
2 c. all-purpose flour
1/2 t. salt
1/2 t. hot pepper sauce
1/8 t. Worcestershire sauce

TEXAS TRIVIA

Are you a Pepper? There's a museum in Waco that tells the story of Dr Pepper, and no, there's not a period after Dr in the name. A young pharmacist, Charles Alderton, invented the syrup for the first soda pop in 1885. When in Waco, check it out and, yes, of course, there's a soda fountain.

CRISPY SWEET PICKLES

ANN BROWN
WINNSBORO, TX

A wonderful recipe found in my mother's 50-year-old cookbook.
If you can't find slaked lime at your grocery, look for pickling lime…
it's the same ingredient with a different name.

7 lbs. cucumbers, sliced
2 gal. water
2 c. slaked lime
2 qts. white vinegar
4-1/2 lbs. sugar
3 T. canning salt
1 t. celery seed
1 t. whole cloves
1 t. mixed pickling spice
3-inch cinnamon stick
14 1-pint canning jars
and lids, sterilized

1 Combine the first 3 ingredients in a large mixing bowl; cover and set aside for 24 hours, stirring occasionally. Drain and rinse until the water runs clear; soak cucumbers in ice water for 3 hours. Drain. Mix the remaining ingredients together; pour over cucumbers. Let stand overnight.

2 Pour cucumber mixture into a large stockpot; bring to a boil. Reduce heat and simmer for 35 minutes; stir often. Pack in sterilized jars leaving 1/2-inch headspace; wipe rims. Secure lids and rings; process in a boiling water bath for 10 minutes. Set jars on a towel to cool; check for seals.

Makes 14 jars

FESTIVE CHICKEN ENCHILADA DIP

JEANNINE ENGLISH
WYLIE, TX

Terrific served with crispy corn tortilla chips.

1 Mix cheeses together until well blended; add garlic, chili powder, cumin, oregano, paprika and cayenne pepper. Mix well; stir in remaining ingredients. Cover and refrigerate overnight.

Serves 12

- 2 8-oz. pkgs. cream cheese, softened
- 1 c. shredded Cheddar cheese
- 1 t. garlic, minced
- 1 T. chili powder
- 1 t. ground cumin
- 1 t. dried oregano
- 1 t. paprika
- cayenne pepper to taste
- 3 boneless, skinless chicken breasts, cooked and chopped
- 1 bunch fresh cilantro, chopped
- 4 green onions, chopped
- 10-oz. can diced tomatoes with green chiles

BLUE RIBBON IDEA

A festive container for chips or snack mix on a potluck table! Simply tie a knot in each corner of a bandanna, then tuck a bowl of goodies into the center.

GLAZED COCKTAIL SAUSAGES

**JANICE DORSEY
SAN ANTONIO, TX**

Put these savory sausages in your slow cooker the morning of the big football game...they'll be ready by kickoff!

2 16-oz. pkg's. mini
  smoked sausages
1 c. apricot preserves
1/2 c. maple syrup
2 T. bourbon or 1 to 2 t.
  vanilla extract

1 Combine all ingredients in an ungreased 3-quart slow cooker. Cover and cook on low setting for 4 hours.

Serves 16 to 20

TEXAS SALSA

**VICKIE
GOOSEBERRY PATCH**

This salsa is great with chips or with grilled meats. Make it ahead of time and have it at the ready!

2 14-1/2 oz. cans stewed
  tomatoes
1/4 c. canned diced
  green chiles
1/2 onion, chopped
juice of 1/2 lime
1 t. garlic, minced
3 T. fresh cilantro,
  chopped
1 t. chili powder
1/8 t. salt

1 Place all ingredients in a blender or food processor. Pulse on low to desired consistency. Cover and chill until serving time.

Makes 16 servings

FRESH FRUIT SALSA

RUTH VEAZEY
SAN ANTONIO, TX

This is such a sweet and fresh salsa! It pairs well with cold cuts or a plate of favorite cheeses.

1 Combine apples, kiwi, strawberries, orange juice, zest, brown sugar and apple jelly; cover and refrigerate.

2 Sprinkle sugar and cinnamon over the tortillas; place on an ungreased baking sheet. Bake at 325 degrees until warmed; remove from oven and let cool. Serve with salsa.

Makes 5 cups

2 apples, peeled, cored and diced

2 kiwi, peeled and diced

1 c. strawberries, hulled and sliced

1/2 c. orange juice

zest of one orange

2 T. brown sugar, packed

2 T. apple jelly

sugar and cinnamon to taste

10-1/2 oz. pkg. flour tortillas, cut into triangles

sugar and cinnamon to taste

GORILLA BREAD

BRENDA HUGHES
HOUSTON, TX

Don't let the cream cheese get too soft before you cut it into cubes...it's much easier to deal with when it's cold and right out of the refrigerator.

1/2 c. sugar
1 T. cinnamon
2 c. brown sugar, packed
1 c. butter
2 12-oz. tubes
  refrigerated biscuits
8-oz. pkg. cream cheese,
  cut into 20 cubes
1-1/2 c. walnuts, coarsely
  chopped and divided

1 Mix sugar and cinnamon; set aside. Melt brown sugar and butter in a saucepan over low heat, stirring well; set aside. Flatten biscuits; sprinkle each with 1/2 teaspoon sugar mixture.

2 Place a cream cheese cube in center of each biscuit, wrapping and sealing dough around cream cheese. Set aside. Spray a 12-cup Bundt® pan with non-stick vegetable spray; sprinkle 1/2 cup nuts in bottom of pan.

3 Arrange half the biscuits in pan. Sprinkle with half the sugar mixture; pour half the butter mixture over top and sprinkle with 1/2 cup nuts. Repeat layers with remaining biscuits, sugar mixture, butter mixture and nuts. Bake at350 degrees for 30 minutes. Let cool 5 minutes; place a plate on top and invert.

Serves 20

STRAWBERRY-LEMONADE PUNCH

CASSIE HOOKER
LA PORTE, TX

We make this delicious punch for bridal showers, baby showers and other get-togethers. Everyone loves it!

1 In a large pitcher, combine frozen juices, cold water and strawberries. Stir well; cover and chill if not serving immediately. At serving time, add ginger ale and stir gently. Serve immediately.

Makes one gallon

6-oz. can frozen
  lemonade concentrate,
  thawed

6-oz. can frozen limeade
  concentrate, thawed

6-oz. can frozen orange
  juice concentrate,
  thawed

3 c. cold water

2 10-oz. pkgs. frozen
  sliced strawberries,
  thawed

2 ltrs. ginger ale, chilled

SOUTHERN SENSATION

CHARLEEN MCCARL
SAN ANTONIO, TX

This recipe has been handed down in my family in Louisiana for many years. It is a wonderful, unexpected flavor and so simple to prepare!

1 In a bowl, combine onions, pecans, cheese and hot sauce. Add just enough mayonnaise to bind everything together. Transfer to a serving bowl. Cover and chill overnight for the best flavor. Serve with an assortment of crackers or chips for scooping.

Makes 8 to 10 servings

1 c. green onions, finely
  chopped

1 c. toasted pecans,
  finely chopped

1 c. finely shredded
  Parmesan cheese

1/8 t. hot pepper sauce,
  or to taste

1/2 to 3/4 c. mayonnaise

assorted crackers or
  chips

ITALIAN EGGPLANT STICKS

KAREN PILCHER
BURLESON, TX

Serve with lots of salsa, sour cream and warm marinara sauce.

3 eggplants, peeled
1 c. Italian-seasoned dry
  bread crumbs
1 t. salt
1 t. pepper
3 eggs
1/4 c. milk
oil for deep frying

1 Cut eggplants into 3"x1/2" sticks; place in ice water for 30 minutes. Drain; set aside. Combine bread crumbs, salt and pepper; set aside. Blend eggs and milk together in a shallow bowl; dip eggplant sticks in egg mixture. Coat sticks with bread crumbs; arrange on a baking sheet. Cover; chill for 30 minutes. Heat one-inch depth oil in a deep skillet; add eggplant sticks.Cook until golden on both sides, about 2 minutes. Remove to drain on paper towels.

Serves 6

SPINACH-ARTICHOKE DIP

DIANE COHEN
THE WOODLANDS, TX

I've been making this yummy dip for get-togethers for years.

2 8-oz. pkgs. cream
  cheese, softened
1/2 c. mayonnaise
14-oz. can artichoke
  hearts, drained and
  chopped
10-oz. pkg. frozen
  chopped spinach,
  thawed and drained
1/2 c. grated Parmesan
  cheese
1 clove garlic, minced
snack crackers, cut-up
  vegetables

1 Place cream cheese and mayonnaise in a bowl. Beat with an electric mixer on medium speed until well blended. Add remaining ingredients except crackers and vegetables; mix well.

2 Transfer mixture to a greased 9" pie plate. Bake, uncovered, at 350 degrees for 20 to 25 minutes, until lightly golden. Serve with crackers or vegetables.

Makes 16 servings

LYNDA'S SPINACH-FETA DIP

LYNDA MCCORMICK
BURKBURNETT, TX

*This is a favorite dip enjoyed with bread cubes or crackers.
Try garnishing with some farm-fresh chopped tomatoes too.*

1 Combine yogurt, cheeses, sour cream and garlic in a food processor. Process until smooth, scraping sides once. Spoon yogurt mixture into a bowl; stir in spinach, dill and pepper.

2 Cover and refrigerate for several hours, until chilled. Let stand for 10 minutes at room temperature before serving. If desired, garnish with additional dill; serve with chips.

Makes 2 cups, serves 8

8-oz. container Greek yogurt
3/4 c. crumbled feta cheese
1/4 c. cream cheese, softened
1/4 c. sour cream
1 clove garlic, pressed
1-1/2 c. baby spinach, finely chopped
1 T. fresh dill, minced, or 1 t. dill weed
1/8 t. pepper
Optional: additional minced fresh dill
pita or bagel chips

TEXAS TRIVIA

Enchilada gravy is a real thing.
Cheese enchiladas are made with processed
or Cheddar cheese and shredded onions.
The topping is a cross between brown
gravy and enchilada sauce, referred to as
enchilada gravy.

MINI SPINACH & BACON QUICHES

VICKIE
GOOSEBERRY PATCH

These are an elegant addition to a special brunch buffet that can be assembled the night before and refrigerated.

1/4 c. onion, diced

2 t. canola oil

10-oz. pkg. frozen chopped spinach, thawed and drained

1/2 t. pepper

1/8 t. nutmeg

2 slices bacon, crisply cooked and crumbled

15-oz. container ricotta cheese

8-oz. pkg. shredded part-skim mozzarella cheese

1/4 c. grated Parmesan cheese

3 eggs, beaten

1 In a skillet over medium heat, cook onion in oil until tender. Add spinach and seasonings; stir over medium heat about 3 minutes or until liquid evaporates. Remove from heat; stir in bacon and cool. Combine cheeses in a large bowl. Add eggs; stir until well blended. Add cooled spinach mixture; stir until well blended.

2 Divide mixture evenly among 12 lightly greased muffin cups. Bake at 350 degrees for 40 minutes or until filling is set. Let stand 10 minutes; run a thin knife around edges to release. Serve warm.

Makes 12 servings

PINEAPPLE-PECAN CHEESE SPREAD

CYNDE SONNIER
MONT BELVIEU, TX

This is a delicious, fast-fix recipe and always yummy with fresh veggies or pieces of toasted whole-grain bread. The combination of the sweet crushed pineapple and the spicy chiles and red peppers is just perfect!

1 In a large bowl, beat cream cheese until smooth. Add Cheddar cheese, 3/4 cup pecans, pineapple, chiles, red pepper and garlic powder; beat until thoroughly combined. Transfer to a serving dish. Cover and refrigerate. When ready to serve, sprinkle with remaining pecans.

Serves 8

- 2 8-oz. pkgs. cream cheese, softened
- 1-1/2 c. shredded Cheddar cheese
- 1 c. chopped pecans, toasted and divided
- 3/4 c. crushed pineapple, drained
- 4-oz. can chopped green chiles, drained
- 2 T. roasted red peppers, chopped
- 1/2 t. garlic powder

BLUE RIBBON IDEA

Serving appetizers before dinner? Offer small bites like marinated garlic olives that will sharpen guests' appetites but not fill them up.

PECAN BITES

HOPE DAVENPORT
PORTLAND, TX

These sweet bites don't even need frosting.

1 c. brown sugar, packed
1/2 c. all-purpose flour
1 c. chopped pecans
2/3 c. butter, melted and
  slightly cooled
2 eggs, beaten

1 Combine sugar, flour and pecans; mix well and set aside. In a separate bowl, stir together butter and eggs; mix into flour mixture. Spoon batter into greased and floured mini muffin cups, filling 2/3 full. Bake at 350 degrees for 22 to 25 minutes. Cool on a wire rack.

Makes about 1-1/2 dozen

STUFFED JALAPEÑOS

CARLA WHITFIELD
BONHAM, TX

I wanted to make stuffed jalapeños for my husband. I had never made them before and he always enjoyed them when other people made them. So I came up with this...he loves them!

10 large jalapeño
  peppers
1-1/2 c. shredded
  Cheddar cheese
2 12-oz. cans chicken,
  partially drained
1-1/4 oz. pkg. taco
  seasoning mix
10 slices bacon

1 Cut each jalapeño pepper across the top; cut a slit and open up pepper. Remove seeds and membranes; set aside. In a bowl, combine cheese, chicken and taco seasoning; mix well. Stuff peppers with mixture. Wrap each with a bacon slice; use a wooden toothpick to fasten.

2 Place peppers on an ungreased baking sheet. Bake at 325 degrees for 40 to 45 minutes, until peppers are soft and bacon is chewy.

Makes 10 servings

MONTEREY MUSHROOM SQUARES

JO ANN
GOOSEBERRY PATCH

These cheesy squares are irresistible! Mix & match different kinds of mushrooms and cheeses for variety.

1 Separate rolls into 2 long rectangles. Press into the bottom and 1/2-inch up the sides of a lightly greased 13"x9" baking pan. Toss mushrooms with melted butter; spoon over dough.

2 Sprinkle with remaining ingredients. Bake, uncovered, at 375 degrees for 20 to 25 minutes. Cut into squares; serve warm.

Makes 2 dozen

8-oz. tube refrigerated crescent rolls

2 c. sliced mushrooms

1/4 c. butter, melted

1/2 c. shredded Monterey Jack cheese

1/2 t. dried oregano

1/4 t. onion salt

OH! THAT TEXAS HEAT!

The hot-o-meter on many Texas foods is determined by the type of chiles used in preparation. It's important to NEVER touch your eyes or your nose after working with chiles. When it comes to fresh chiles, the choices are many:

ANAHEIM CHILE — Not too hot, with a somewhat sweet flavor.

HABANERO CHILE — Be warned. It's super-hot, but with a fruity flavor.

JALAPEÑO CHILE — There are very hot and very mild versions; used in many dishes.

POBLANO CHILE — Not too hot, with a mild, earthy taste.

SERRANO CHILE — Be careful, as it packs some powerful heat.

CHAPTER FIVE

LONE STAR

Desserts

NO MATTER WHAT STATE
YOU HAIL FROM, THERE IS
ALWAYS ROOM FOR DESSERT.
GO AHEAD AND GRAB
SOME YUMMY CALORIES
AND ENJOY A LITTLE SWEET
SOMETHING AT THE END OF A
TEXAS-SIZE MEAL.

CARROT CAKE

KAREN MORAN
NAVASOTA, TX

Crushed pineapple adds extra moistness to this scrumptious carrot cake.

3 c. all-purpose flour
2 t. baking powder
2 t. baking soda
1 t. salt
2 t. cinnamon
4 eggs
2-1/2 c. sugar
1-1/2 c. oil
1 t. vanilla extract
2 carrots, peeled and grated
15-1/4 oz. can crushed pineapple, drained
1-1/2 c. chopped nuts
Cream Cheese Frosting

1 Stir together first 5 ingredients in a medium bowl. Beat eggs and next 3 ingredients in a large mixing bowl at medium speed with an electric mixer until smooth. Add flour mixture, beating at low speed until blended. Fold in carrots, pineapple and nuts.

2 Pour batter into 3 greased and floured 9" round cake pans. Bake at 350 degrees for 25 to 30 minutes, or until a toothpick inserted in center comes out clean. Cool in pans on wire racks 10 minutes. Remove from pans and cool completely on wire racks. Spread Cream Cheese Frosting between layers and on top and sides of cake.

Serves 16

CREAM CHEESE FROSTING:

2 8-oz. pkgs. cream cheese, softened
1/2 c. butter, softened
2 16-oz. pkgs. powdered sugar, sifted
2 t. vanilla extract
1 c. chopped nuts

1 Beat cream cheese and butter at medium speed with an electric mixer until smooth. Gradually add powdered sugar, beating at low speed until light and fluffy. Stir in vanilla and nuts.

Makes 6-3/4 cups

CHERRIE-O CREAM CHEESE PIE

CHRISTINA RODGERS
EL PASO, TX

My grandmother made this yummy pie for every holiday and every special occasion. It is so easy and so good!

1 Combine cream cheese and condensed milk in a bowl. Beat with an electric mixer on high speed until creamy. Add lemon juice; stir until well blended. Stir in vanilla; pour into crust. Cover and refrigerate for 2 to 3 hours, until set. Just before serving, top with pie filling.

Serves 6 to 8

8-oz. pkg. cream cheese, softened

14-oz. can sweetened condensed milk

1/3 c. lemon juice

1 t. vanilla extract

9-inch graham cracker crust

21-oz. can cherry or blueberry pie filling

ROCKY ROAD BROWNIES

SHERYL WHITED
AUSTIN TEXAS

Add a cup of Spanish peanuts too...yummy!

1 Prepare brownie mix as directed on package: spread in a greased 13"x9" baking pan. Sprinkle one cup marshmallows and one cup chocolate chips over batter. Bake according to package directions. Remove from oven; sprinkle with remaining marshmallows and chocolate chips. Let cool completely before cutting into squares.

Makes 2 to 3 dozen

19-1/2 oz. pkg. fudge brownie mix

2 c. mini marshmallows, divided

12-oz. pkg. semi-sweet chocolate chips, divided

CHOCOLATE CHIP-OAT COOKIES

TRACEY TEN EYCK
AUSTIN, TX

This recipe was handed down to me by my mother, who is now ninety-five. She made the best homemade cookies ever!

1 c. butter
3/4 c. brown sugar, packed
3/4 c. sugar
2 eggs
1 t. hot water
1-1/2 c. all-purpose flour
1 t. baking soda
1 t. salt
12-oz. pkg. semi-sweet chocolate chips
2 c. long-cooking oats, uncooked
Optional: 1 c. nuts, finely chopped
1 t. vanilla extract

1 In a large bowl, beat butter until soft. Gradually add sugars, blending until light and fluffy. Add eggs, one at a time, beating well after each addition. Stir in hot water.

2 In a separate bowl, mix together flour, baking soda and salt; gradually add flour mixture to butter mixture. Stir in chocolate chips, oats and nuts, if desired; mix thoroughly. Add vanilla and blend well. Drop by 1/2 teaspoonfuls onto greased baking sheets. Bake at 375 degrees for 8 to 10 minutes, until tops are golden.

Makes 4 dozen, serves 24

KITCHEN TIP

Be sure to let your butter soften before beating with sugar so no lumps will form. You'll get perfect results every time!

CREAMY BANANA PUDDING

ELIZABETH COX
LEWISVILLE, TX

This is our favorite pudding...a quick dessert to make anytime. Sometimes I sprinkle a few fresh blueberries on top of the finished pudding. Yummy!

1 Process cream cheese, pudding mix, 2-1/2 cups milk and vanilla in a food processor or blender until smooth. Pour into a large bowl; whisk in remaining milk.

2 Whisk whipped topping into pudding mixture. Layer crushed vanilla wafers, banana slices and pudding mixture in a 4-quart casserole dish. Top with additional whipped topping and vanilla wafers, if desired. Chill at least 4 hours before serving.

Serves 10 to 12

1-1/2 c. cream cheese, softened

1-1/2 5.1-oz. pkgs. instant vanilla pudding mix

4-1/2 c. milk, divided

1-1/2 t. vanilla extract

12-oz. container frozen whipped topping, thawed

12-oz. pkg. vanilla wafers, coarsely crushed

4 bananas, sliced

Optional: additional whipped topping and vanilla wafers, broken into large pieces

COCONUT-SOUR CREAM CAKE

JO ANN
GOOSEBERRY PATCH

*This rich cake is so beautiful and white. Cut it into small pieces
and serve with fresh fruit. Everyone always loves it!*

- 18-1/4 oz. pkg. butter-recipe cake mix
- 16-oz. container sour cream
- 2 c. sugar
- 4 c. sweetened flaked coconut
- 1-1/2 c. frozen whipped topping, thawed

1 Prepare and bake cake mix according to package directions, using 2 greased and floured 9" round cake pans. Slice each cake layer horizontally in half, using a long serrated knife.

2 Combine sour cream, sugar and coconut in a bowl; stir well. Cover and chill 1-1/2 hours. Reserve one cup sour cream mixture. Spread remaining sour cream mixture between layers.

3 Fold whipped topping into reserved sour cream mixture. Spread on top and sides of cake. Place cake in an airtight container. Cover and chill at least 8 hours.

Makes 12 servings

TOO-EASY TOFFEE CHEESECAKE

ANDREA HEYART
AUBREY, TX

*This simple cheesecake is a snap to pull together, yet tastes like
you spent hours in the kitchen!*

- 2 8-oz. pkgs. cream cheese, softened
- 2/3 c. brown sugar, packed
- 1 t. vanilla extract
- 2 eggs
- 1 c. chocolate-covered toffee baking bits, divided
- 9-inch graham cracker crust

1 In a bowl, combine cream cheese, brown sugar and vanilla. Beat with an electric mixer on medium speed until blended. Add eggs, one at a time, beating after each addition. Stir in 3/4 cup toffee bits; pour mixture into crust. Bake at 350 degrees for 35 to 40 minutes, until center is set. Sprinkle with remaining toffee bits while cheesecake is still warm. Cool; cover and refrigerate at least 3 hours.

Makes 6 to 8 servings

CHOCOLATE OAT CUPCAKES

JOSHUA LOGAN
VICTORIA, TX

The oat flour in these cupcakes makes them more dense and the cocoa and dark chocolate chips make them so chocolatey. This will become your favorite chocolate cupcake!

1 In a bowl, combine flour, brown sugar, baking cocoa, baking powder, baking soda and salt. Mix well; gently stir in chocolate chips. In a separate large bowl, combine remaining ingredients except garnish; mix well. Add flour mixture to zucchini mixture; stir only until well combined.

2 Spoon batter into muffin cups sprayed with non-stick vegetable spray, filling cups 2/3 full. Sprinkle oats on top of muffins, if desired. Bake at 400 degrees for 18 to 20 minutes, until a toothpick tests clean. Cool muffin tin on a wire rack for 10 minutes; remove muffins from tin.

Makes 12 servings

2 c. oat flour
1/3 c. brown sugar, packed
1/3 c. baking cocoa
2 t. baking powder
1/2 t. baking soda
1/2 t. salt
3/4 c. dark chocolate chips
2/3 c. zucchini, finely grated
1 c. skim milk
3 T. honey
2 egg whites, beaten
Garnish: oats

DATE-FILLED COOKIES

ADELE PETERMAN
AUSTIN, TX

A recipe handed down from my grandmother...it's a family favorite!

1-1/3 c. sugar
2/3 c. shortening
1/4 c. milk
1 t. vanilla extract
2 eggs
3-2/3 c. all-purpose flour
2-1/2 t. baking powder
1/2 t. salt

1 Blend sugar and shortening until light and fluffy; add milk, vanilla and eggs. Combine flour, baking powder and salt. Add to sugar mixture; blend well. Divide dough in half; wrap and chill at least one hour.

2 Roll out dough and cut into 2-inch rounds with a cookie cutter or glass. Place half of dough rounds on baking sheet, fill with 1/4 teaspoon Date Filling. Top with remaining dough rounds and press edges together with a fork. Bake at 400 degrees for 8 to 10 minutes, until slightly browned. Remove from pans to wire racks to cool.

Makes about 3-1/2 dozen

DATE FILLING:
1 T. all-purpose flour
1/2 c. sugar
1 c. dates, finely chopped
1/2 c. water

1 Combine flour and sugar in a medium saucepan; stir in dates and water. Cook over low heat, stirring constantly, until mixture thickens.

Makes about 3/4 cup

DAFFODIL BANANA CRUSH PUNCH

CHRISTI PERRY
GAINESVILLE, TX

*My grandmother sent me off to college with this recipe…
it was always a hit at every gathering!*

1 Combine all ingredients except ginger ale; mix well. Divide into 8 large plastic zipping freezer bags; freeze. Remove bags from freezer 3 to 4 hours before serving. Pour into punch bowl; add 3 quarts of chilled ginger ale.

Serves 40

6 c. water

4 c. sugar

32-oz. can pineapple juice

6-oz. can frozen orange juice concentrate, thawed

1/2 c. lemon juice

6 bananas, mashed

3 qts. ginger ale, chilled

TRAVELING FUDGE

PAULA BONCHAK
BONHAM, TX

I have been sending goodies to my overseas military family members so that they can have a taste of home. This arrives fine, and everyone loves it. I thought I'd share the recipe for Traveling Fudge so that others can send some to their families.

1 Bring sugar, milk and butter to a rolling boil in a heavy 5-quart Dutch oven over medium heat, stirring until sugar dissolves. Cook, stirring constantly to prevent scorching, to the soft-ball stage, or 234 to 243 degrees on a candy thermometer. Remove from heat. Stir in chocolate chips and marshmallow creme until melted and well blended. Add vanilla and nuts, if desired.

2 Pour into a buttered 13"x9" baking pan. Cool completely and cut into squares. Store in an airtight container.

Makes 2-1/2 to 3 pounds

3 c. sugar

1 c. evaporated milk

1/2 c. butter

12-oz. pkg. semi-sweet chocolate chips

1 c. marshmallow creme

1 t. vanilla extract

Optional: 1 c. coarsely chopped pecans or walnuts

DOUBLE PEANUT COOKIES

JO ANN
GOOSEBERRY PATCH

For all the peanut lovers out there! Smooth peanut cookies with crunchy roasted peanuts...too good.

1 c. all-purpose flour
1/2 t. baking soda
1/2 c. shortening
1/2 c. creamy peanut butter
1/2 c. sugar
1/2 c. brown sugar, packed
1 egg, beaten
1/2 c. salted dry-roasted peanuts

1 In a bowl, mix together flour and baking soda; set aside. In a separate large bowl, beat shortening and peanut butter until well blended. Add sugars; beat until fluffy. Beat in egg. Stir in flour mixture until well blended; stir in peanuts.

2 Drop by rounded teaspoonfuls, 2 inches apart, onto ungreased baking sheets; flatten slightly. Bake at 350 degrees for 10 to 12 minutes, until lightly golden. Cool on baking sheets for about 5 minutes; remove to a wire rack to cool completely.

Makes 3 dozen

FAMILY FAVORITE FROSTING

NICHOLE SULLIVAN
SANTA FE, TX

At our house, we slather this frosting on everything from cakes to cookies...it also makes a yummy filling for homemade cookie sandwiches. A friend calls it "birthday cake frosting" because she says it tastes just like the frosting on the cakes you get at the bakery.

16-oz. pkg. powdered sugar
1 c. butter-flavored shortening
2 T. water
2 t. vanilla extract

1 Place all ingredients in a large bowl. Beat with an electric mixer on low speed to combine. Increase speed to medium; beat for 5 full minutes. At first it won't look much like frosting, but keep the mixer going for the full 5 minutes.

Makes enough to frost a 2-layer cake or a 13"x9" sheet cake

GERMAN CHOCOLATE PIE

PAULINE RAENS
ABILENE, TX

Our family loves this yummy pie filled with all kinds of texture. It tastes like a German chocolate cake but cuts like a pie. What could be better?

1 Melt chocolate and butter over low heat until smooth; let cool. Beat eggs, flour, sugar and vanilla for 3 minutes at high speed with an electric mixer until blended. Pour chocolate mixture over egg mixture and beat 3 more minutes. Stir in pecans and coconut.

2 Pour into a well-greased 9" pie plate. Bake at 350 degrees for 28 minutes. Cool. Just before serving, garnish with whipped cream, shaved chocolate and pecans.

Serves 6

2 1-oz. sqs. sweet baking chocolate
1 c. butter
3 eggs
2 T. all-purpose flour
1 c. sugar
1 t. vanilla extract
1 c. pecans, chopped
1/2 c. flaked coconut
Garnish: whipped cream, shaved chocolate, pecans

FROSTY BUTTER PECAN CRUNCH PIE

LISA JOHNSON
HALLSVILLE, TX

Sometimes I add some chopped pecan pieces on top of the pie along with the candy bar pieces. So yummy!

- 2 c. graham cracker crumbs
- 1/2 c. butter, melted
- 2 3.4-oz. pkgs. instant vanilla pudding mix
- 2 c. milk
- 1 qt. butter pecan ice cream, slightly softened
- 8-oz. container frozen whipped topping, thawed
- 2 1.4-oz. chocolate-covered toffee candy bars, crushed

1 Combine graham cracker crumbs and melted butter in a medium bowl; pat into an ungreased 13"x9" baking pan. Freeze until firm.

2 In a large bowl, beat pudding mix and milk at medium speed with an electric mixer until blended, about one minute. Fold in ice cream and whipped topping; spoon over chilled crust. Sprinkle with candy bar pieces; freeze. Remove from freezer 20 minutes before serving.

Serves 12 to 15

GERMAN CHOCOLATE POUND CAKE

WANDA FREEMAN
KRUM, TX

This is my tried & true dessert for every potluck and social...it's so easy to make, bakes up beautifully and tastes scrumptious. Everyone loves it!

1 Spray a Bundt® pan with non-stick vegetable spray; place on a baking sheet and set aside. In a bowl, combine dry cake mix, eggs, water and oil. Stir until well blended; beat with an electric mixer on medium speed for 2 minutes. Slowly beat in frosting until blended. Pour into prepared pan.

2 Bake at 350 degrees for about 55 minutes, testing for doneness with a toothpick. Allow cake to cool in pan for 5 minutes; invert onto a serving plate and allow to cool completely. Dust with powdered sugar before serving.

Makes 10 to 12 servings

18-1/2 oz. pkg. German chocolate cake mix
3 eggs, beaten
1 c. water
1/3 c. oil
16-oz. can coconut-pecan frosting
Garnish: powdered sugar

KITCHEN TIP

Did a little yolk escape when you separated your egg? Not to worry! Use the eggshell to fish it out. The yolk will naturally be attracted to it.

SIGNATURE CHOCOLATE CREAM PIE

**KAY LITTLE
DIANA, TX**

This is an easy, tried & true recipe that I have passed down to my daughter, Jennifer. It is just what you want in a chocolate pie...a rich, intense chocolate filling dressed up with whipped cream. And the filling takes only a few minutes to make!

3 egg yolks
1-1/2 c. whole milk
1 c. sugar
2 T. all-purpose flour
2 T. cornstarch
3 T. baking cocoa
1/4 t. salt
2 T. butter
1 t. vanilla extract
9-inch pie crust, baked
Sweetened Whipped
  Cream

1 In a large bowl, beat egg yolks and milk with an electric mixer on low speed until blended. In a separate bowl, mix sugar, flour, cornstarch, cocoa and salt. Add to egg mixture; blend well. Pour mixture into a microwave-safe bowl. Microwave on high setting for 6 to 8 minutes, until thickened, stirring well at 2-minute intervals. Add butter and vanilla; stir well. Immediately pour mixture into baked pie crust. Cool to room temperature; cover and refrigerate for one hour. Serve topped with dollops of Sweetened Whipped Cream.

Serves 6 to 8

**SWEETENED
WHIPPED CREAM:**

2 c. whipping cream,
  chilled
1/2 c. powdered sugar
1 t. vanilla extract

2 With an electric mixer on medium-high speed, beat cream until soft peaks form. Add powdered sugar and vanilla; beat until stiff peaks form.

GOOEY BUTTER COOKIES

ANDREA HEYART
AUBREY, TX

These cookies have been a Christmas tradition in my family for at least 20 years now. Whoever is in charge of baking always knows to double or triple the recipe. No matter how many are on hand, they will all be devoured well before New Year's Eve!

1 In a large bowl, combine all ingredients except powdered sugar. Beat with an electric mixer on high speed until well mixed. Cover and chill for at least 30 minutes.

2 Scoop chilled dough into one-inch balls; roll in powdered sugar. Place on parchment paper-lined baking sheets. Bake at 350 degrees for 9 to 12 minutes, until golden; a little underdone is better than overdone. Let cool. Sprinkle with additional powdered sugar, if desired.

Makes 2 dozen

15-1/4 oz. pkg. golden butter cake mix

8-oz. pkg. cream cheese, softened

1 egg, beaten

1/2 c. butter, softened

1 t. vanilla extract

Optional: powdered sugar

CHOCOLATE CAPPUCCINO BROWNIES

**JO ANN
GOOSEBERRY PATCH**

Chewy and chocolatey together, with a touch of coffee flavor...delicious!

1/2 c. butter, melted

1 c. brown sugar, packed

2 T. instant coffee granules

3 eggs, slightly beaten

1 t. vanilla extract

1/2 c. brewed coffee, cooled

1 t. baking powder

1/2 t. salt

1-1/4 c. all-purpose flour, sifted

1/3 c. plus 1 T. baking cocoa

1 c. chopped walnuts

1 c. semi-sweet chocolate chips

Garnish: powdered sugar

1 In a bowl, combine butter, brown sugar and coffee granules; blend well. Add eggs, vanilla and cooled coffee; stir. In a separate bowl, combine baking powder, salt, flour and cocoa; add to butter mixture. Stir in walnuts and chocolate chips, mixing well.

2 Pour batter into a greased 13"x9" baking pan. Bake at 350 degrees for 25 to 30 minutes. Allow brownies to cool. Cut into squares. Dust with powdered sugar before serving.

Makes 1-1/2 to 2 dozen

KITCHEN TIP

Plump up raisins and dried cranberries for baking and they will be soft and tasty. Cover them with boiling water and let stand about 15 minutes, then drain well and pat dry.

MUGGA'S DUMP CAKE

JILL JONES
RICHMOND, TX

When my son was small, he couldn't say "grandmother" so he called my grandmother "Mugga." This is a wonderful dessert she made and it always reminds me of her. Scrumptious served warm with vanilla ice cream!

1 Add pineapple with juice to a greased 13"x9" baking pan; top with pie filling. Sprinkle with sugar and dry cake mix; press down with your fingers. Drizzle melted butter over top. Bake at 350 degrees for 45 minutes. Cut into squares; serve warm.

Serves 12

11-oz. can crushed
  pineapple
21-oz. can apple or peach
  pie filling
1/2 c. sugar
18-1/2 oz. pkg. yellow
  cake mix
1/2 c. butter, melted

OATMEAL-RAISIN BARS

JESSICA HENDERSON
WICHITA FALLS, TX

This is my husband's favorite treat. He'd love it if we always had some on hand! It's even low in fat...what more could you ask for?

1 Line the bottom and sides of a 13"x9" baking pan with aluminum foil, allowing 2 to 3 inches to extend over sides. Lightly grease foil and set aside. Stir together dry cake mix, oats and raisins in a large bowl. Stir in 3/4 cup applesauce with a fork until mixture is crumbly and dry ingredients are moistened. Press half of mixture into bottom of pan. Stir together remaining applesauce and spice in a separate bowl; gently spread over mixture in pan. Sprinkle with remaining cake mix mixture.

2 Bake at 375 degrees for 30 minutes, or until top is golden. Cool completely in pan on a wire rack. Lift cooled bars from pan, using foil as handles. Place on a cutting board and cut into bars.

Makes 2 dozen

18-1/2 oz. pkg. yellow
  cake mix
2 c. quick-cooking oats,
  uncooked
1/2 c. raisins
1-3/4 c. applesauce,
  divided
1/4 t. apple pie spice

ROCKY ROAD-PEANUT BUTTER CANDY CUPS

VICKIE
GOOSEBERRY PATCH

Everyone loves the combination of peanut butter and chocolate. The crispy rice cereal and marshmallows just add a little more yumminess!

11-oz. pkg. peanut butter and milk chocolate chips
2 T. creamy peanut butter
1 c. crispy rice cereal
1 c. mini marshmallows
3/4 c. unsalted roasted peanuts, chopped

1 Microwave peanut butter and milk chocolate chips in a large glass bowl on high one to 2 minutes, until melted, stirring every 30 seconds. Stir in peanut butter until well blended.

2 Stir in rice cereal, mini marshmallows and chopped peanuts. Spoon mixture by heaping tablespoonfuls evenly into mini paper candy cups. Chill one hour or until firm.

Makes 3 dozen

KITCHEN TIP

Chocolate chips, raisins and nuts won't sink to the bottom of the bowl if you toss them in a tablespoon of flour before adding to the batter.

SHORTBREAD FINGERS

ALICE JOY RANDALL
NACOGDOCHES, TX

I've made this recipe for over 40 years. It is delicious and very easy.

1 Combine flour, sugar, butter and vanilla in a bowl. Work with your fingers until well blended and a soft dough forms. Press dough evenly into an ungreased 8"x8" baking pan. Pierce well all over with a fork. Bake at 350 degrees for 25 minutes, or until lightly golden. Cut into 32 bars; sprinkle with powdered sugar. Cool completely in pan on a wire rack.

Makes 32 cookies

1-1/2 c. all-purpose flour
1/3 c. sugar
1/2 c. butter, softened
1/2 t. vanilla extract
Garnish: powdered
 sugar

DULCE DE LECHE BARS

ANDREA HEYART
AUBREY, TX

This rich chocolate and caramel dessert makes a wonderful take-along to cookie exchanges and holiday parties! Dulce de leche is caramelized sweetened condensed milk...you'll find it in the Hispanic aisle or with the dessert toppings.

1 In a bowl, combine dry cake mix, eggs and applesauce. Stir until mixture forms a sticky dough. In a 13"x9" baking pan, spread and pat down 3/4 of mixture; set aside. Place chocolate chips, dulce de leche and butter in a microwave-safe bowl. Microwave on high for one to 2 minutes, until melted. Stir well to combine; spread over first layer. Place large spoonfuls of remaining cake mix mixture on top, flattening and spreading as much as possible. Bake at 350 degrees for 20 to 25 minutes, until golden. Cool completely before cutting into bars.

Makes 10 to 14

18-1/2 oz. pkg. spice cake
 mix
2 eggs, beaten
1/3 c. unsweetened
 applesauce
6-oz. pkg. semi-sweet
 chocolate chips
14-oz. can dulce de leche
1/4 c. butter

SLICE-OF-COMFORT PIE

DIANA DIAZ DE LEON
SAN ANTONIO, TX

I hope you like this no-bake pie as much as I do! Halve the ingredients to make one pie.

16-oz. container frozen
  whipped topping,
  thawed
1 c. chopped pecans
14-oz. can sweetened
  condensed milk
16-oz. can crushed
  pineapple, drained
2 9-inch graham
  cracker pie crusts

1 Mix first 4 ingredients together; divide and pour equally into pie crusts. Place in the freezer overnight or until frozen.

Makes 2 pies; each serves 8

SNOWBALLS

HOPE DAVENPORT
PORTLAND, TX

Covered in coconut flakes…there'll be no snowball fights with these!

1 c. semi-sweet chocolate
  chips
1/3 c. evaporated milk
1 c. powdered sugar
1/2 c. chopped walnuts
1-1/4 c. sweetened flaked
  coconut

1 Combine chocolate chips and milk in a double boiler; cook over hot water until chocolate melts. Stir to blend well.

2 Remove from heat; stir in powdered sugar and nuts. Cool slightly. Form into one-inch balls; roll in coconut.

Makes about 2 dozen

SOFT PUMPKIN COOKIES

CONNIE HILTY
PEARLAND, TX

My family prefers a soft cookie and these are their favorite ones!

1 Combine flour, baking powder, baking soda and cinnamon in a bowl. Beat together sugar and butter in a separate bowl until blended. In another bowl, stir pumpkin, egg and vanilla until smooth. Gradually add flour and sugar mixtures and stir well.

2 Drop by rounded tablespoonfuls onto greased baking sheets. Bake at 350 degrees for 15 to 18 minutes, until edges are firm. Cool on baking sheets for 2 minutes, then transfer to a wire rack. Cool completely; drizzle Glaze over cookies.

2-1/2 c. all-purpose flour
1 t. baking powder
1 t. baking soda
1-1/2 t. cinnamon
1-1/2 c. sugar
1/2 c. butter, softened
1 c. canned pumpkin
1 egg, beaten
1 t. vanilla extract
Glaze

1 Combine ingredients in a small bowl; mix until smooth.

Makes 2-1/2 dozen, serves 30

GLAZE:
1 c. powdered sugar
2 T. skim milk
1 t. butter, melted
1 t. vanilla extract

TEXAS 2-STEP APPLE CRISP

JENNIFER SWARTZ
SMITHVILLE, TX

The slow cooker tenderizes these apples while creating a perfectly crisp topping...resulting in a grand finale for any meal.

6 cooking apples, peeled, cored and sliced
1-1/2 c. all-purpose flour
1 c. brown sugar, packed
1 T. cinnamon
1/2 t. nutmeg
1/4 t. ground ginger
1/2 c. butter, softened
Garnish: vanilla ice cream, whipped topping, maraschino cherries

1 Arrange apple slices in a lightly greased 4- to 5-quart oval slow cooker; set aside.

2 Combine flour and next 5 ingredients in a bowl; mix well. Sprinkle flour mixture over apples, pressing down lightly. Cover and cook on low setting 5 hours or until apples are tender. Garnish with your favorite toppings.

Serves 6 to 8

VANILLA WAFER CAKE

MARGIE SCOTT
WINNSBORO, TX

This is so easy to make but is so delicious! I like to serve it with chocolate topping.

1 c. butter
2 c. sugar
6 eggs
12-oz. pkg. vanilla wafers, crushed
1 c. pecans, chopped
1/2 c. milk
1 t. vanilla extract

1 Beat butter and sugar until light and fluffy. Add eggs, one at a time, beating well after each addition. Add vanilla wafers, pecans, milk and vanilla. Pour into a greased and floured Bundt® pan. Bake at 325 degrees for 1-1/2 hours. Let cool in pan; remove from pan and cool completely on a wire rack.

Serves 12 to 16

TELEPHONE COOKIES

JULIE GAVIN
SAN ANTONIO, TX

We've been making these scrumptious no-bakes for nearly 50 years now. They came about through my grandma's telephone eavesdropping. She shared a party line with her neighbors as they lived out in the country. One day when Grandma wanted to use the phone, she picked up the receiver and heard the neighbor lady giving out a recipe. She quickly wrote down the ingredients and directions, but never caught the name of the recipe. We love these cookies...kids love to make them too!

1 Combine one cup powdered sugar, butter, peanut butter and cereal in a large bowl. Mix with your hands and form into walnut-size balls. Place in a plastic freezer container; freeze.

2 To make frosting, combine remaining powdered sugar and milk until smooth. Dip frozen cookies into frosting and roll in coconut. Keep stored in the freezer in a sealed container.

Makes 6 dozen

2 c. powdered sugar, divided

2 T. butter, softened

1 c. creamy peanut butter

1-1/2 c. crispy rice cereal

3 T. milk

1 c. sweetened flaked coconut

INDEX